Counseling Native American Indians

Insights from Conversations with Beaver

Cognella Series on Advances in Culture, Race, and Ethnicity

Counseling Native American Indians

Insights from Conversations with Beaver

"GENE" HIGHTOWER AND "BEAVER" BERRY

University of California, Berkeley

Bassim Hamadeh, CEO and Publisher
Amy Smith, Project Editor
Jess Estrella, Senior Graphic Designer
Alisa Munoz, Licensing Associate
Natalie Piccotti, Senior Marketing Manager
Kassie Graves, Vice President of Editorial
Jamie Giganti, Director of Academic Publishing

ISBN: 978-1-5165-4030-3 (pbk) / 978-1-5165-4031-0 (br)

This book is dedicated to the memory of my uncle, Roy Hightower, a kindly man who was born and raised in Wetumka Oklahoma (Muscogee Creek Nation) at the beginning of the 20th century and instilled in me his love for Indian people. It is also dedicated to the memory of my grandmother, Sudie Williams, who taught me at an early age the importance of generosity and integrity. I am indebted to Beaver for asking me to interview him and put his ideas in print.

Gene Hightower

I dedicate this book to those recovering alcoholics who helped me find the Red Road to sobriety and to all recovering alcoholics everywhere.

Beaver

Acknowledgments

I am grateful for the assistance I have received from the Native American Studies Program and the Townsend Center of the University of California, Berkeley. I am also deeply appreciative of the financial support received from the Woodfish Foundation of San Francisco.

Reverend William Modlin offered editorial assistance and has been a valued counselor since my undergraduate days at Harvard College. My thanks also to Professor Wesley Leonard, Larry Hernandez, Joel Schrag, Ignacio Camacho, and Yohanna Foto for their technical assistance. A special thanks to Professor Arthur Blue, a founding member of The Society of Indian Psychologists, for his encouragement of this project. I am also deeply indebted to Professor Joseph Trimble for his guidance and support in bringing this manuscript to completion. Most importantly, I acknowledge Beaver for being a superb mentor and guide. He taught me how to walk the Red Road.

Contents

List of Figures

Foreword by Russell Thornton

Russell Thornton
Distinguished Professor of Anthropology, UCLA

Gene Hightower has written a sensitive, compassionate story of a remarkable man. Beaver, aka Turner Arthur Berry Jr., was a Choctaw Indian man from Oklahoma who struggled with alcoholism but eventually achieved sobriety, in large part through his own Indian spiritualism. From then, Beaver devoted his life to helping others conquer the demons of alcoholism, especially those in California, where he had moved. Along the way, Beaver became a model of "an Indian path through life." He achieved highly respected status as an American Indian elder and spiritual leader in several urban tribal Indian communities in California. Many looked to him for guidance out of the darkness of intergenerational historical trauma that impacts Indian communities and toward the light of "Indianness." Until his death, Beaver helped other American Indians, not only with their struggle to maintain sobriety but also with the challenge of living a life grounded in traditional Indian cultural values in modern times.

The book was written as Beaver's last request to Hightower to put his insights in writing. He does an admirable job of putting Beaver's ideas into print. Hightower also skillfully weaves into the story his mastery of the literature on Native American Studies; as a result, Beaver's story is put in the context of the academy and makes an important scholarly contribution. Hightower writes of himself as well as Beaver as perhaps only an Indian psychologist could. The result is a story of two men that captures essential aspects of their lives and their development as Indian individuals.

I recommend this short book to anyone seeking to understand what it means and does not mean to be an Indian in today's American society.

Foreword by Joseph E. Trimble

Joseph E. Trimble
Distinguished University Professor Professor of Psychology
Western Washington University

Traditional indigenous healers embrace and practice the deep meaning and influence of spirit, the sacred, and place in all relationships. Many also know that conventional contemporary psychological counseling and psychotherapy are slowly considering the importance of including the spiritual, the sacred, and the meaning of place in the healing process. Many healers also acknowledge the genuine possibility that centuries-old traditional healing practices are more powerful, if not more so, than contemporary approaches to dealing with mental health problems. Someone must tell their stories with their permission. Gene Hightower is one who has been asked by a traditional healer to tell one of those stories.

About four decades ago, three of my close American Indian friends and I spent a few days in a traditional lodge in a remote area of South Dakota. Two Native healers, holy men, accompanied us. The healers extended us the invitation to be with them because they wanted us to hear their stories. We were there to learn about their ways of healing along with the traditions, ceremonies, customs, and ways of their world. Through one story after another, the healers thoroughly engaged us in the deep mysteries of traditional practices we had heard about over the years, but we knew little about their deeper historical meaning. During the day, we would walk around the area by ourselves or in groups talking, reflecting, and probing deeply into the wisdom unfolding in the stories we were hearing. We prepared and cooked meals together, with family members often joining us in the chilly evenings, a small fire always burning in the center of the lodge.

On the morning of our last day with the healers, they asked us to explain how we psychologists provided "healing" for those in need. The clinical psychologist in our group—a person with considerable experience working in mental health settings focused on providing services for different multicultural clients—described how the client would sign up for a session, what took place in the first and subsequent sessions, how the "counseling" unfolded, and generally what would happen in each session. Another friend added a few features of the relationships between the mental health helper and the client. The healers listened intently, though often with puzzled expressions.

Following our detailed descriptions, the healers began asking the following questions: Do you personally know the clients? Why do they have an appointment with you for an hour each week? Do they always show up? Why do you talk and talk with them and them with you? How do you know you helped or healed them? Do you ever see them again? Do you ask the spirits to help you as you talk with them? Do spirits sometimes come in the room where you're sitting? Why do you sit when the two of you talk? Why aren't others present when you talk with one another? Do you ask their ancestors to join you? Is the room where you're sitting clean and clear of evil and bad spirits? Are both of you clean and clear of anything bad that may interfere with the talking and healing? Do the clients prepare for each meeting by sweating, praying, meditating, and fasting? Do counselors also prepare this way for each meeting with the client? Why do you take notes? Does the talking occur in a sacred place? What happens to the two of them after the client is healed?

We attempted to answer each of their surprising questions. With each response, we focused more on what we were saying to them and the possibility that their questions were more profoundly meaningful and appropriate than we realized. We also knew on that day that conventional counseling and psychotherapy were a long way from including the spiritual, the sacred, or the meaning of place in the healing process and considering the real possibility that centuries-old traditional healing practices were as powerful, if not more so, than contemporary approaches to mental health.

Recognition and acknowledgement of what was at the heart of the healers' probing questions and concerns that day wouldn't come to the evolving mental health fields until much later. In 2003, the American Psychological Association published a set of multicultural guidelines that gave attention to changes in society at large and to the emerging data about "the different needs of unique individuals and groups historically marginalized or disenfranchised within and by psychology based on their ethnic/racial heritage and social group identity or membership" (American Psychological Association, 2003, p. 377). The overarching goal of the guidelines was to provide psychologists with a rationale for the urgency to address multiculturalism and diversity in education, training, research, practice, and organizational change.

The APA guidelines set an agenda for the emergence of the field of multicultural psychology with an emphasis on cross-cultural counseling and psychotherapy. Culturally competent counselors were encouraged to give attention to the spiritual dimension of the client's life and consider the profound influence of religious, spiritual, and transpersonal beliefs, practices, and development over the life span. To this end, the practitioners are encouraged to use a client's spiritual beliefs in the pursuit of the client's therapeutic goals. Similarly, counselors are asked to carefully and thoughtfully focus on connections—similarities and differences among religion, spirituality, and the transpersonal—and to describe beliefs and practices in a cultural context. They are encouraged to articulate a client's self-exploration of personal beliefs and to explain various models of spiritual development across a client's life span. Counselors also are encouraged to demonstrate sensitivity to and acceptance of a variety of spiritual expressions from the client. And, importantly, the guidelines recommended that counselors acknowledge the limits of their understanding of a client's spiritual and deeply cultural expression and demonstrate appropriate referral skills.

There is a strong growing belief among culturally competent practitioners that inclusion of spirituality and collaboration with traditional healers and elders in the counseling process and intervention programs create better outcomes. Therapy offered in a manner congruent with the traditional values and spirituality of the clientele can reverse the historical trend to forego traditional lifeways and thoughtways and assimilate dominant cultural ways and worldviews exclusively to get better and healthier. With counseling and psychotherapy aligning with culture, there is now the possibility of receiving treatment supportive of one's own culture, beliefs, and spirituality.

In this book, the reader will discover that a traditional American Indian healer knows a great deal about what works best for those who seek guidance, assistance, and healing. Beaver fully understands that the relational styles of healers are comparable with what they know works effectively in building and sustaining positive counseling relationships. These styles are common among effective counselors and therapists who are endowed with certain personal characteristics that promote positive relationships with clients, regardless of cultural background. Indeed, this is the foundation of any healing or helping process. Characteristics such as empathy, genuineness, warmth, respect, and availability are likely to be effective in any setting or ethnocultural community.

These same characteristics often exemplify the spiritual healers in numerous indigenous communities. The Inupiat Alaska Native counseling psychologist Catherine Swan Reimer, for example, collected information from Inupiat members in an Alaska Native village concerning the characteristics they found desirable in a healer. Her respondents indicated that a healer is (a) virtuous, kind, respectful, trustworthy, friendly, gentle, loving, clean, giving, and helpful; (b) thoroughly strong; (c) one who works well with others by becoming familiar with people in communities; (d) one who has good communication skills; (e) respected because of his or her knowledge; (f) substance free; (g) one who knows and follows the culture; and (h) one who has faith and a strong relationship with the Creator (Reimer, 1999, p. 60).

Advances in multicultural psychology are assembling the pieces of a multicolored quilt that are giving us a much broader outlook on spirituality, culture, and psychology. And Gene's confident and authoritative written voice is one of the quilt's patches. His long-awaited book is beautifully crafted, clearly written, convincing, and logically organized, complete with a wealth of thought-provoking material organized in an accommodating style

Through Beaver's voice, experiences, and insights, Gene Hightower convincingly argues that the inclusion of indigenous spiritual worldviews in mental health intervention and treatment will produce better client outcomes and better relationships among people no matter where they live. Anyone who carefully and thoughtfully studies these pages will come out a richer, well-informed person who will view spirit, the sacred, place, and connectedness through a discerning lens.

References

American Psychological Association (2003). Guidelines on multicultural education, training, research, practice, and organizational change for psychologists. *American Psychologist, 58*(5), 377–402.

Reimer, C. S. (1999). *Counseling the Inupiat Eskimo.* Westport, CT: Greenwood.

Preface

One day as Beaver and I were discussing traditional American Indian spiritual practices, he said, "It is time for you to get more serious about your spirituality." His comment surprised me. Beaver knew that I prayed regularly and occasionally participated in sweat lodge ceremonies. Only a year before, he had consecrated my prayer pipe. "A couple of those guys have asked me to put them up on the hill. We are going next month," he said. I knew Beaver was suggesting that I should also go on a vision quest.

I expressed my fears. I thought it might be hard on my body if I went up. I had been badly injured in a car accident a decade earlier. I was left with a ruptured disc in my lower back and body heat-regulation problems. I was not sure my back could handle the hard ground. I was afraid I might get a chill in the nighttime mountain air (especially after opening up my pores in the sweat lodge ceremony that I'd be expected to participate in prior to going up on the hill). I balanced these considerations against the possible benefits. Beaver had always said, "Going up on the hill is one's time alone with Creator. That's your one-on-one time with God to see what His will is for your life." I knew that many people have had powerful life-changing visions and/or received spirit helpers. I had also heard of people who ran down hillsides in terror after frightening encounters with powerful spirits. I decided to give it a chance.

The time to go up on the hill arrived. It was late September, when the weather is unpredictable in Northern California. It can be warm and sunny one day and cool and rainy the next. We met in a wooded, hilly area to the east of Hollister, California, a 3-hour drive from my home in San Francisco. The traffic leaving the metropolitan area had been unusually heavy, and I arrived near sunset; I had planned to arrive around noon. Beaver told me that it was too late for me to go up that day. He decided we should wait until the next morning. Members of the Wolf Spirit Gourd Clan Society were there to support people who were going "up on the hill." We had a great campfire dinner that night, and the Gourd Clan Society sang sacred songs to support those already on vision quests.

Upon arising the next morning, I went looking for Beaver. I found him sitting and chatting amicably with the other Gourd Society members. He told me not to eat breakfast or drink anything. He said my fast had already begun at sunrise. He asked his helpers to prepare the sweat lodge. The sweat lodge is a dome-like structure made of willow and covered with cloth or hides. When its front flap is closed, it is completely dark inside. In the sweat lodge ceremony, participants sit around a pit filled with heated stones. Water is periodically poured over these stones to produce steam. Sacred herbs placed on the stones create healing incense. The leader of the ceremony sings in a rhythmic fashion, calling for the intervention of spirit powers. The sweat lodge ceremony is a purification ceremony in which participants seek to return to the womb of Mother Earth and be reborn.

Before going to the sweat lodge ceremony, I had mentioned to Beaver that I was worried about overheating and having my pores be too open to cool mountain winds. I suffer from a medical condition that causes me to get cold easily. He smiled, looked me earnestly in the eyes, and said, "Don't worry, Gene. You will be protected." He motioned to some of the other society members to come take me up to the place he had picked out for me. He told them how he wanted the grounds prepared when we arrived. In his late 70s and walking with a cane, Beaver preferred to let assistants walk vision seekers up the hill. He waved me off and laughed, saying, "Let's see if we can heat you up today!" He also said, "I'll be praying for you." I thought to myself, *I sure as hell am going to need prayers!*

After a long, arduous climb up the trail, we got to the spot that Beaver had picked for me to fast and pray. I immediately fell in love with it because it afforded a broad view of the surrounding countryside. One could see for miles in every direction. I have always loved scenic vistas and was happy that I had not been placed in a secluded, shady, wooded spot. Some of the others were in such locations (of course, that may have been right for them).

The Gourd Clan Society members prepared the area as Beaver had instructed. The elder of this group told me that if I got too hot, it was okay to strip down. I told him it was unlikely that I'd do that, as I wear heavy clothing throughout the year. I tend to become cool easily. They reminded me of Beaver's instructions. I was not to leave the sacred circle they had created until they came back to get me. They said they would occasionally check on me from a distance, but that I would not see them. I was told not to worry. They then left me alone.

The day became a sizzler. I was surprised! The temperature climbed to what felt like 90 or 100 degrees by high noon. I thought I would pass out. I was already thirsty and hot from the sweat ceremony and the climb up the hill. I had not had any water to drink that day. There were no trees immediately adjacent to my spot. There were trees a few yards away, but Beaver had warned me not to leave the sacred circle for any reason. He said I was protected as long as I stayed within its confines but was at the mercy of evil forces should I step outside of it, even for a moment.

Beaver had told me to notice any animals—no matter how small—that came near or into my circle that day. I crouched next to a bush that was in my space. It did not offer much shade, but it was a help. As I sat there, I started noticing ants crawling up and down its leaves and branches. They became fascinating to me. Some of the ants were red, and others were black. Suddenly, an ant that was half red and half black appeared! I was told this ant and I were the same. I realized in that moment how completely natural it was to be what I am, a Black Indian (a person of mixed African American and American Indian descent who identifies with Indian cultural ways).

Near sunset, as the air began to cool down to a more comfortable 80 degrees or so, I felt free to move about my space. Beaver had instructed me to pray with the pipe whenever the mood hit me. Suddenly, I felt a strong urge to pray. I loaded my pipe with tobacco and offered it, as I normally do, to the four directions. However, something very different happened this time. From each of the four cardinal directions, spirits came to me. From the East, a young warrior dressed in bright yellow buckskin approached me. He was fringed with bright yellow and red feathers. He looked like a grass dancer. He told me to call on him whenever I needed renewal. He said he would help me become more youthful and joyful. From the South, there appeared a very wise and knowledgeable maiden dressed in reddish-brown buffalo-hide clothing. She walked toward me carrying the sacred pipe. The words "sister friend" came to my mind. She spoke to me for a long time and answered many questions. From the West came a blue-skinned man with long, thick black hair. His appearance reminded me of dark-skinned Indian men I had seen in New Mexico and Arizona. He said little other than that he was a guardian from the spirit world of the ancestors. Lastly, from the North, there came a late-middle-aged medicine man wearing a buffalo-horn hat. He was strong, reassuring and ethical. He knew a lot about medicine and curing. After this prayer session, I felt great peace. I have not related all the details of my vision, just enough to give the reader a sense of what I experienced.

The night was beautiful. The full moon lit up the countryside. Hundreds of stars shone brightly in the clear night sky. It was relatively warm, and I was quite comfortable. I have had few such tranquil moments. I felt one with all of Creation. I have heard stories of people who had run screaming from their spots at night in the middle of their vision quests, but fortunately, this was not to be my experience.

A little past sunrise, I was surprised to see the Gourd Clan Society members coming for me. They said it was time to pack up and go down. When we returned to camp, Beaver said he had sent for me, as he knew that I had received my vision and there was no need to stay longer. He asked to speak to me privately in his tent. He then explained to me what he understood my vision to mean and its implications for my future life. He also told me I could not reveal to others what he told me.

For all who read this book, may it serve you in a good way.

Introduction

FIGURE I.1   Beaver.

T he idea for this book came about in the spring of 2002. Beaver and
I were sitting and talking one day, and he said to me that he would
be 80 years old in the upcoming year and felt like he wanted to leave his
ideas on traditional Indian spiritual values for others to read. He said he
was going to ask his grandson, who was an undergraduate in college, to
type up what he had to say. I suggested to him that I could help with this
project if he wanted. I put forth the dubious proposition that, as a published psychologist and visiting professor in Native American Studies at
UC Berkeley, I might have a better handle on how to approach the task of
writing a book about his life and teachings. He accepted my offer. I was
told later by Indian friends that Beaver had played an old Indian trick
on me by playing "the elder in need of assistance." It is not unusual for
an Indian elder to ask in such a fashion. A friend told me when that his
Indian grandmother wanted a ride to town, she would sit in a chair next to
the road until someone in the family asked her if she needed a ride. In any
event, Beaver told me that several people had asked to write a book about

1

his teachings and he had turned them down. He said that when he met me, he knew I was the person who was supposed to write the book on his teachings.

We decided on an interview format. This text is based on approximately 7 hours of taped interviews with Beaver and written commentaries by people whom Beaver had helped or mentored over the years. Beaver read the final transcript of our interviews and the resultant manuscript, and he made deletions, corrections, or amplifications where he felt necessary. I expanded my initial discussion of the relevant literature about 10 years after his death.

Beaver was an enrolled member of the Choctaw Nation of Oklahoma. He was raised in Oklahoma in the 1920s but moved to California in the late 1950s. Beaver joined the newly developing intertribal community in Northern California. Many Indian people came to cities in California and elsewhere through the federal government's Urban Indian Relocation Program, which was then in force. Once Beaver got over his addiction to drugs and alcohol, he became a substance abuse counselor and dedicated his life to helping other Indians find sobriety and form a better relationship between themselves and the Creator. Many people consider Beaver a medicine man, but he refused to apply that term to himself. He would say he just prayed for people when they needed help.

Beaver's life is a remarkable story of overcoming blatant racism in Oklahoma; being subjected to the cruel Indian boarding school system; surviving mortal combat in World War II and subsequent post-traumatic stress; and undergoing the breakup of his first marriage and the consequent loss of his much-loved children. In this book, he tells how these events led to a life of substance abuse and antisocial behavior and how returning to the traditional Indian values taught to him by his uncle, a medicine man, led to his recovery. He also details how he started a substance abuse treatment program based on traditional American Indian values in order to help the American Indian community. A respected elder, he describes in detail what "traditional American Indian values" truly are (especially in the urban American Indian intertribal context) and why it is important for American Indian people to follow pan-Indian "traditional" values. He spent his later life doing all he could to help the Native American Indian community. Native American Indians will be referred to in this text as "American Indians" (in the vernacular of First Nations people of the United States).

I was very close to Beaver for 8 years. I originally heard of him from a Micmac Indian friend who told me there was a highly respected medicine man of my tribe (I am mixed Choctaw, Cherokee, and Creek Indian as well as

African American on my father's side) in the Central Valley whom I should try to meet. I was told he was the head of a Gourd Clan Society. The Gourd Clan Society is a fraternal organization whose roots are in the buffalo culture of the Southern Plains Indian people (Boyd, 1981).[1] I was also told that he frequently led sweat lodge ceremonies and took people on vision quests. There has been much discussion about the power of medicine Indian spiritual practices.[2] I decided to give Beaver a call and ask to meet with him.

Beaver was a slender, short man with a warm, age-wizened smile and a dignified demeanor. He bore a strong resemblance to Chief Dan George, the actor who played Old Lodge Skins, the kindly grandfather and Cheyenne chief in the movie *Little Big Man*. At our first meeting, I was impressed by Beaver's great humility. He refused to be referred to as a "medicine man." He would say, "I'm just a recovering alcoholic" with a warm twinkle in his eyes. I was captivated by Beaver's quiet dignity and warmth.

Beaver was not one to sit still. He was always on the move. Beaver loved working in his house garden, which was full of flowers, herbs, and vegetables. He grew sage and gave it away. He liked to be active, always tinkering with something. He loved animals and had four dogs, several cats, a pig, and a goat as pets. He lived with his son, daughter-in-law, and three grandchildren. He was devoted to his family and was constantly looking after the welfare of his teenage grandchildren, who adored him.

I have many warm memories of sitting outside Beaver's farmhouse, located near Turlock, California and situated on an isolated country road deep in an orchard area. For more than 7 years, we met on a biweekly basis. In warm weather, we sat outside, surrounded by orchards, talking and praying, and when it was cold, rainy, or hot, we prayed inside by his potbelly stove. He was a good listener and a wise, down-to-earth, practical counselor.

My father's family were Black Indians. My father's family is involved in Stomp Dance ceremonies in Oklahoma. My mother has no family oral history of Indian ancestry, however she has taken DNA tests that indicates that she has Indian ancestry. She does not know if this ancestry came from her mulatto mother or from her North Dakota Caucasian father (who had a grandfather named "Gray Eagle"—certainly an Indian sounding name). My father (now deceased) never took DNA testing saying that he did not need scientific tests to know he had Indian ancestry. He thought such testing a waste of good money. However one of his sisters was a participant in a genetic research study at the University of Oklahoma. Results indicated that my aunt has Indian ancestry. My father's older brother, Uncle Roy, said our family lived among the Muscogee Creek as they were the most accepting of African/Indian mixed race people. He said "We were never treated any differently than anyone else in the tribe." A wise medicine man once said to me "People are like rivers their origins are often unclear. Who knows for sure who all their ancestors were a thousand years ago?"

I came to Beaver relatively unschooled in traditional Indian values, although I had participated in a few ceremonies and read a lot about Indian culture. Beaver guided me to deeper insights about the true meaning of Indian spirituality, as only a wise Indian elder could. He taught me the way of the sacred pipe and how to use it to pray for the good of others. Beaver also helped me get over my insecurities about being part of the Indian world. He spoke to me about the long involvement of mixed-blood people in the Choctaw tribe. He encouraged me to accept my own worth as equal to other Indians—or anyone else, for that matter. He was an excellent mentor! A Ojibwa medicine man whose sweat I attended also spoke to me on this issue. He went around the circle and spoke to each person in the sweat lodge as if he was reading their mind. He encouraged me to put away any doubts, as "You are one of us." Everyone in the sweat said, "Welcome home!" to me and hugged me after the sweat ended. I was deeply touched. Beaver built on this experience.

While Beaver was supportive and kind, he was also capable of being confrontational. He always challenged me, and others, to do better. He was a great role model of integrity and ethical practice. He repeatedly said, "Do the right thing for the right reason and take the flak," "Be yourself," and "Do what you can to help another human being." He encouraged me to believe that any difficulty would build character if I came to the right understanding of it. This perspective has helped me greatly over the years. I found it particularly reassuring when Beaver would say, often in a group setting, "I am teaching you what my grandfathers have taught me. I hope you all will pass it on someday to your grandchildren." Considering his age, this meant he was passing down teachings from elders who lived in the 19th Century! Beaver was loved and respected by many in the Indian community because he gave so generously of himself for more than 40 years. I have seen him allow homeless and distraught people to stay at his house for weeks, never asking for a penny. I have seen him fast and pray for someone who was sick and ask for no more than a handshake.

We attended numerous events together over the years, traveling across the United States to attend Indian spiritual ceremonies. He traveled to Fort Hall, Idaho, to support me when I participated in the Sun Dance (although he was not a Sun Dancer). It was a blistering-hot summer (temperatures over 100 degrees), yet Beaver was there every day, praying for me and even gathering herbs to press against my face to help me stay cool. This would have been a challenging activity for even a man younger than Beaver (who was 76 at the time).

Wherever we went, Indians and non-Indians alike always seemed to take an immediate liking to Beaver. He had a striking, charismatic presence and a warm, folksy style. I often heard people remark that he was "a real Indian." Once, a group of teenaged Indian boys on the Blackfoot reservation called him an "old-time Indian." He always remained humble in spite of the high regard he received.

I invited Beaver to speak to Native American Studies classes I taught at UC Berkeley and Stanford University. Several students reported later that they felt their lives had changed for the better after meeting him. I am a psychologist and have brought a few patients to visit Beaver. They have remarked that just one pipe ceremony with Beaver had changed their lives for the better and that they felt privileged to have met him. I invited him to lead a staff prayer ceremony when I was director of mental health services at Native American Health Services in Oakland, California. My coworkers reported being deeply moved by the things Beaver said and did that afternoon. This was a very special ceremony because Ana Coelho, another pipe carrier who was a close friend of Beaver's, was also present and sang prayer songs in a beautiful way. At numerous times, I have been with others in Beaver's prayer ceremonies; I always saw people smile as they left, as though a burden had been lifted from their shoulders. He had the rare gift of making others feel appreciated and understood within just a few minutes of meeting him.

I do not want to leave readers with the impression that Beaver was all "sweetness and light." He could be direct, forceful, and unyielding, He had no problem letting people know when he thought they were screwing up. However, he did not hold grudges. He often said, "Never give up on another human being. People can always change. I did." Still, he was not gullible or easily fooled by others. He saw others for who they are. We were once sitting together at a powwow when an Indian man approached Beaver and asked if he was a medicine man. Beaver told the man he was not, adding, "I am just an old man." The man who had approached us then exclaimed, "I am a medicine man!" Beaver said, "No, I don't think you are" with a smile. The man turned and quickly walked away. I could not keep from laughing.

Beaver gave tirelessly of himself. Until the end of his life at age 80, he would fast for 4 days and pray for the health of sick individuals. He took people on vision quests and stayed with them for most of a week until they received their vision. He conducted sweat lodge ceremonies. He gourd danced at powwows. He never turned down anyone who came to him for help, and he never charged for his help, although people often made donations. He always stressed the importance of helping people when they came to him for help and not putting them off until a more convenient time. He once told me, "When you carry the sacred pipe in the right way, you treat everybody as your friend." This is the story of a remarkable spiritual man, a man whom most saw as a wise Indian elder.

Beaver led ceremonies that cured many of physical and psychological problems. He referred to himself as a certified substance abuse counselor and an Indian elder who prayed for others. He lived very much in the way Katz (2017) describes the role of the Indian elder/healer:

> Indigenous elders earn their status as a result of being acknowledged by their community as a person who has lived a long life and is able to reflect on their lives and generate valued meanings and understandings. … Elders are considered sources of traditional, spiritually infused cultural teachings. They have the ability to perform important ceremonies. … They are always working toward being honest, trustworthy, generous, empathetic and humble. … They work to help younger people who are overwhelmed with life return to physical, emotional, mental and spiritual balance. … (with the great modern-day migration of tribal First Nations people to metropolitan areas) urban elders and healers are essential.[3]

In mainstream psychology today, there is greater recognition of the important role spirituality can play in counseling, as seen in the work of Professor Lisa Miller, who is director of clinical training at Columbia University's Psychology Department. She argues that direct experience of the sacred promotes optimal individual psychological health and community well-being.[4] Joan Koss-Chioino argues that personal transformation occurs when transcendent spiritual experiences are incorporated into consciousness.[5] There is also discussion of "transpersonal psychology."[6] These perspectives are congruent with the work of elders like Beaver.

Notes

1   Boyd, M. (1981). *Kiowa voices: Ceremonial dance, ritual and song.* Fort Worth, TX: Christian University Press.

Lassiter, L. (1998). *The power of Kiowa song.* Tucson, AZ: University of Arizona Press.

Meadows, W. (1999). *Kiowa, Apache, and Comanche military societies.* Austin, TX: University of Texas Press.

2 Brown, J., & Black Elk. (1989). *The sacred pipe.* Norman, OK: University of Oklahoma Press.

Brochac, J. (1993). *The Native American sweat lodge.* Freedom, CA: Crossing Press.

3 Katz, R. (2017). *Indigenous healing psychology: Honoring the wisdom of first peoples.* Rochester, VT: Healing Arts Press.

4 Miller, L. (2012). *The Oxford University Press handbook of psychology and spirituality.* New York: Oxford University Press.

5 Koss-Chioino, J., & Hefner, P. (2006). *Spiritual transformation and healing: Anthropological, theological, neuroscience, and clinical perspectives.* Lanham, MD: Altima Press.

6 Krippner, S. (2014). *Varieties of anomalous experience* (2nd ed.). Washington, DC: American Psychological Association.

1

Counseling Native American Indians

An Overview

It is very difficult to counsel American Indians without some appreciation of the historical impact of European colonizers on tribal communities. Early Massachusetts colonists would have perished had it not been for assistance from Indian people (Wampanoag). The Pilgrims who had come to America looking for religious freedom suppressed Indian religions and customs.[1] Euro Americans continued to outlaw American Indian religious practices until 1978, when the federal American Indian Religious Freedom Act was passed. In spite of the U.S. Constitution's guarantees of religious freedom, Indian people were routinely punished for practicing their religions during the first 200 years of the American republic. As Vine Deloria (2003) astutely observed, "The churches devoted themselves wholeheartedly to converting the people. … Missionaries soon became one of the more vocal forces in demanding that tribal political activity be suppressed, since it was apparent to them that the religious and political forms of life could not be separated."[2] Indians were sent to jail for praying as their ancestors had done for centuries[3].

Since the inception of the English colonies, Indian nations were consistently commanded to move further west in order to free land for White settlement. The military might of the American government, combined with a lack of immunity to European diseases, led to a massive decrease in the population of Indian nations. The policy of removing Indians to "Indian lands" was strictly enforced after the American Revolution. One of the American government's largest land grabs occurred after the passage of the Indian Removal Act in 1830. This federal law mandated that Indian nations east of the Mississippi relocate to the new Oklahoma

Indian Territory. Southeastern American Indians, such as the Cherokee and Choctaw (elders and children included), were forced to surrender their prosperous farmlands and personal belongings prior to walking thousands of miles on the infamous "Trail of Tears" (known to the Cherokee as "the trail where we cried") to the new territory and a life of poverty. This occurred even though the United States Supreme Court had ruled that the Cherokees should not be forced to relocate. President Andrew Jackson, a former army general renowned as an "Indian fighter" (but who was considered a terrorist by many Indians during his days as a general), announced that he had no intention of obeying opinions of the Supreme Court that were contrary to his Indian removal policy. Many died in route to Oklahoma. There were also the "Great Indian Wars," which were directed against Plains Indians (e.g., the Lakota) and Southwestern tribes (e.g., the Apache) to force their removal from traditional tribal lands.

Today, Indian nations carry the legal status of "Domestic Dependent Nations" managed by the Bureau of Indian Affairs (BIA)—they lost their status as being nations independent from the United States. The BIA reflected the second guiding principle of Indian policy captured in the slogan "Kill the Indian, save the man." This philosophy allowed for the continued physical presence of Indians as long as they became fully assimilated to Euro American cultural ways. This aim justified the forced removal of Indian children from loving homes where they were taught the traditions of their people and their deliverance to sterile government boarding schools where they were abused, neglected, punished for speaking their languages, and taught that they were inferior to White people. Strict military discipline, inadequate diets, poor sanitation and ventilation, and overcrowding caused outbreaks of tuberculosis and pneumonia. Some elders still living today have traumatic memories of these facilities. Teenagers graduated from these schools confused about their identity. They had little experience with stable, nurturing adult role models. When they returned to their tribal communities, most were ill equipped for the demands of adult life. Their own children were often taken away by White social workers who perceived them to be unfit parents. Their children were placed in the adoptive homes of White families. This final assault on the Indian family did not end until the passage of the Indian Child Welfare Act in 1978, which mandates that Indian foster children be placed with Indian families as a top priority.

The stability of Indian communities was also challenged by the Termination Program in the 1950's—under which the federal government reneged on treaty obligations to several tribes—and the Urban Relocation Program of the

1960's, which sought to encourage further assimilation by luring Indians to the big cities with false promises of prosperity. For over a century, American Indian culture, including even constitutionally protected religious freedoms, cultural ceremonial practices, and languages, were actively suppressed by the federal government. There is ample discussion of the legacy of cultural and community suppression of Indians in the literature.[4,5]

These historical atrocities have left a legacy of trauma in the American Indian community. Anxiety, depression, and concomitant substance-abuse/alcohol-abuse related issues—such as suicide, family violence, and auto accidents. Poverty and physical ailments also became widespread problems in Indian communities.[6] American Indians have the highest rate of significant life stress of any ethnic group in the United States (U.S. Commission on Civil Rights, 2004).[6] Some have described this pattern of emotional distress as the "Historical Trauma Response," defined as "the cumulative, emotional and psychological wounding across generations, including the lifespan which emanates from massive group trauma."[7] Others have called it as a "soul wound" assault on Indian self-esteem and dignity.[8] It is held that community-wide psychosocial difficulties—such as grief, anger, and acting-out behavior (such as sexual abuse and addiction)—are the direct result of a genocidal colonization process in the United States. The White clinician who would work with Indians must be cognizant of this history and willing to cope with impersonal anger and suspicion.

Demonstrating an awareness of Indian cultural values and practices is beneficial in overcoming this skepticism about non-Indians. Clinicians who would be helpful must evidence a keen sensitivity to Indian cultural ways; otherwise, they will discover that their American Indian clients usually do not come back after the first session. There are nearly 600 American Indian nations in the United States, all with distinct cultures and histories. Identifying a set of common "Indian values" is challenging. Still, some would argue that there is a commonly shared worldview for American Indians that can be distinguished from the Euro American worldview.

Generally speaking, Indian values are communal and stress relationship to other human beings and the whole of nature. Some commonly enunciated values are generosity, cooperation, community participation, humor, humility, noninterference in others' life direction, listening carefully to others, a preference for observation over explanation, respect for elders and tradition, living in the present, stewardship of nature, and a tendency to incorporate supernatural/spiritual meanings into everyday life.

The non-Indian therapist working with American Indians will need to practice Indian etiquette if they are to be successful. Some suggestions include: avoid interrupting clients when they are speaking, allow for silence between statements (the wait time between sentences is much longer for traditional American Indians than Euro Americans), do not force self-disclosure, find gentle ways to encourage self--expression, avoid interpreting and intellectualizing, do not make judgmental comments as to what the client "should do," show respect (for example, by avoiding direct eye contact), ask permission, express gratitude, never assume privilege, remain flexible about scheduling, be hospitable, show a sense of humor, and demonstrate one's humility. Indian clients would be most comfortable in a physical setting that is welcoming and comfortable; this reflects the Indian cultural value of generosity. They would also prefer clinicians who downplay their status by taking a more democratic, self-disclosing stance. This would reflect the highly valued attitude of humility. Indian clients also prefer therapists who are open to discussing dreams and visions as messages from the spirit world. Indian clients are not likely to return after an initial session if the counselor is dismissive of Indian beliefs and customs.[9]

In traditional Indian societies, feedback is often given in an indirect manner. An elder may attempt to address problem behavior by speaking in general terms in a group setting about individuals who are "acting badly" without naming the perpetrators directly. Most people know who is being discussed, and the individual with the problematic behavior gets the message. Clinical feedback is often given in a narrative, storytelling fashion. As Hays (2008) eloquently writes: "One traditional helping strategy that can be incorporated into mainstream psychotherapy is the practice of storytelling. ... Used as a helping strategy, the speaker does not directly advise the listener, but rather tells a story through metaphor that offers a social message. The speaker is then free to draw a conclusion if he or she is ready to do so." This method is often employed in "talking circle" groups. In these groups, a ceremonial object—such as an eagle feather or staff—is passed around the group. Each participant is permitted to speak without interruption as they hold this ceremonial object. After each member of the group has spoken, the group leader often comments on significant issues that were raised.[10]

Less than 10% of American Indians living today are "full-bloods" (i.e., having no other ancestry than that of their tribal group), and half of those claiming Indian racial ancestry on the 2010 census also claim ancestry from another racial group. While one will find many people in the Indian world who fit the Hollywood image of the Indian with brown skin and straight black hair, one will also see lighter-skinned Indians and Indians with curly hair, blond hair, blue eyes, etc. Some American Indians are mistaken for Euro Americans, Asians, Latinos, or African Americans. Some people see Indian genes as "spreading thin," and others see Indian genes as "spreading out."

The trend toward a racially mixed Indian population will no doubt increase in the future, as 75% of Indian people report being married to non-Indians. While there are tribes, such as the Navajo, in which most of its citizens are primarily descended from Indian people, there are also tribes, such as the Cherokee, that have many members with less than a sixteenth Indian ancestry. In the United States, each tribe sets its own standard for tribal membership. Laws governing Indian status are quite different in Canada and Latin America.

Whites have intermarried with Indians for hundreds of years, and their mixed-race descendants have generally been accepted as tribal members.[11] Southeastern tribes, such as the Creek and Seminole, have intermixed with individuals of African descent since colonial times; indeed, there have been many centuries of intermixing between Indians and Africans. However, they were often denied tribal enrollment even when Indian parents testified that these were their children.[12] In southwestern states, there are many people of mixed Spanish and Indian ancestry who are influenced by both tribal customs and mestizo culture.[13]

Historically, Indian people have generally considered anyone who lived in the community and participated in the tribe's cultural practices to be part of the group.[14] Indeed, some court rulings state that if a person is considered Indian by other Indians, he/she can be considered Indian for *some* legal purposes.[15] The American standard has been to determine Indian status by the amount of Indian ancestry (blood quantum). The federal government (and some states governments) has given tribes the power to set their own criteria for enrollment. Due to out marriage, some enrolled individuals have children who fail to meet individual tribal requirements for enrollment. Given the increasing heterogeneity of the American Indian gene pool due to out marriage the question arises: Are cultural commitment and community involvement better measures of Indian status than blood quantum alone? The issue of racial mixture is a significant one for some American Indian people. This can lead to disputes and charges of racial discrimination when proof of Indian ancestry is demanded.[15]

Insecurities as to whether one is "Indian enough" occur for some Indian people, whether they are enrolled in a recognized tribe or not.[16] Some Indian people focus on what is described as "the empty center." In this scheme, the full-blood Indian who is conversant in his tribal customs/language is seen as the "ideal" Indian; all others fail to measure up. However, even the few who fully fit this ideal are still seen to be somewhat deficient, as, it is argued by some, only the "old-time" Indians of past centuries are "real Indians." Insecurities surrounding Indian authenticity may present as issues in counseling sessions and must be approached gently so as to avoid shaming the client.[17]

The argument that the only "true Indian" is a person who is an enrolled member of a federally recognized tribe would leave many Indians unaccounted for. Today, there are individuals who are members of tribes that were never recognized by the federal government due to opposition from local political interests (as we see in the case of some California tribes). There are tribes that were once recognized by the federal government only to lose their recognition under the federal government's Termination Program in the 1950s. They lost their recognition for no other reason than that federal policy became to abrogate treaty obligations wherever possible. There are also some tribes, such as the Lumbee, who have only recently succeeded at achieving tribal recognition, and other tribes are still seeking federal recognition. Some tribes, such as the Yaqui, straddle the U.S./Mexico border. Tribal members born on the American side of the border are considered American Indian by the federal government, while relatives born on the Mexican side of the border (if they emigrate to the United States) are not. In some tribal communities, political infighting leads to some individuals being "unenrolled" after tribal disputes. The BIA acknowledges that there are many with Indian ancestry who are not "enrolled."

There was a 75% increase in the number of individuals claiming both Indian and Hispanic ancestry on the 2010 census. Some of this increase is the result of immigration, and some of it is due to Latinos increasingly deciding to honor their American Indian ancestry. In general, the 2010 census indicates more individuals identifying as American Indian than on the 2000 census. The increase is more than would be accounted for by new births. Fogelson has noted a trend toward "retribalization" among the current-day descendants of American Indians. This is defined as a returning to traditional Indian cultural roots.[18] This movement may be reflected on the 2010 census. Determining which groups can rightfully claim Indian status is a complex legal/historical and *political* matter.[19]

A key issue in counseling American Indians is determining the extent to which a person has achieved a positive identification with Indian values; this identification plays a crucial role in coping with intergenerational trauma.

The clinician needs to consider whether a client's identity status is traditional, bicultural, assimilated, pan-traditional, or marginal.[20]

The traditional identity style is here defined as the individual who maintains an active involvement in their tribal community and is conversant in their tribal language, religion, and customs. This individual often maintains minimal contact with the larger Euro American society. This person may be uncomfortable working with counselors who are not intimately familiar with his or her tribal culture and may prefer traditional Indian healers.

Bicultural individuals, like traditional individuals, are conversant and comfortable with cultural forms of their tribe, but they are also actively engaged in the mainstream society. Many of these individuals live comfortably in both worlds, often seeing the strengths and weaknesses of both groups. They would likely work well with both traditional healers and culturally sensitive counselors.

Assimilated individuals see themselves as Americans with Indian ancestry (the amount of ancestry notwithstanding) and have little appreciation of American Indian folkways. Some of these individuals are indifferent or even hostile toward Indian cultural forms. They would be most helped by culturally sensitive Euro American therapists who gently encourage more openness to Indian culture.

The pan-traditional individual is one who has made a conscious decision to reclaim a lost Indian ancestry and seeks to learn about American Indian cultural practices, beliefs, and values. They would be open to traditional healers and culturally sensitive therapists—especially ones who are willing to teach them about tribal traditions.

Lastly, there is the individual with a marginal Indian identity. While marginal individuals do not see themselves as White, they have a weak identification with the Indian cultural values. It is said that these individuals "identify with Indian pain," the pain of historical trauma. They are not utilizing the great resources and strengths to be found in the Indian culture. They profit greatly from engagement with more traditional elders and counselors who can teach them about the strengths of their culture.

A counselor may happen upon individuals who decide—with little known Indian community involvement, and no ancestral or genetic ties—that they *must* be Indian. I have seen this in some "New Age" adherents who are convinced they are Indian due to past life experience. They are infatuated with the very powerful "symbol of the Indian."[21] The clinician should help this client explore their need to see themselves as Indian and encourage them to explore their own cultural roots. An Indian medicine woman related to me the story of how a "New Age" young man told her he was just like an Indian. He said he wanted to be one with Nature, so he jumped into a lake. The medicine woman gently told him the difference was that an Indian would ask the lake's permission before jumping in. The lake has its own consciousness. Beaver was open to non-Indians participating in his ceremonies as long as they were sincere in their interests and realized that being in an Indian ceremony did not make them Indian.

Notes

1   Talbot, S. (2006). Spiritual genocide: The denial of American Indian religious freedom from conquest to 1834. *Wicazo SA Review, 21.*
2   Deloria, V. (2003). *Custer died for your sins.* Norman, OK: University of Oklahoma Press.
3   Dejong, D. H. (2007). Unless they are kept alive: Federal Indian schools and health. *American Indian Quarterly, 31.*
4   Smith, H. (2006) *A seat at the table: In conversation with Native Americans on religious freedom.* Berkeley, CA: University of California Press.
    Tafoya, N., & Del Vecchio, A. (2005). Back to the future: An examination of the Native American holocaust experience. In M. McGoldrick, J. Giordano, and N. Garcia-Preto (Eds.), *Ethnicity and family therapy.* New York: Guilford.
5   Arnott, T. (1996). I am the fire of time. In T. Arnott & J. Matthaei (Eds.), *Race, gender and work.* Boston, MA: South End Books.
6   Boyd-Ball, A., Manson, S., Noonan, C., & Beals, J. (2006). Traumatic events and alcohol use disorders among American Indian adolescents and young adults. *Journal of Traumatic Stress, 19.*
    Manson, S. (2005). Social epidemiology of trauma among two American Indian reservation populations. *American Journal of Public Health, 95.*
    Manson, S. (2000). Mental health services for American Indians and Alaska Natives: Needs, use, and barriers to effective care. *Canadian Journal of Psychiatry, 45.*
7   Braveheart, M., Chase, J., Elkins, J., & Altschul, D. (2011). The historical trauma among indigenous peoples of the Americas: Concepts, research, and clinical considerations. *Journal of Psychoactive Drugs, 19.*
8   Duran, E. (2006). *Healing the soul wound.* New York, NY: Columbia University Press.

9   King, J. (2009). Psychotherapy within an American Indian perspective. In M. Gallardo (Ed.), *Intersections of middle identities: A casebook of evidenced based practices with diverse populations*. Florence, KY: Routledge.

Sutton, C., & Broken Nose, M. (2005). American Indian families. In M. McGoldrick, J. Giordano, & N. Garcia-Preto (Eds.), *Ethnicity and Family Therapy*. New York, NY: Guilford.

Deloria, V., Silko, L., & Tinker, G. (2003). *God is red*. Golden, CO: Fulcrum.

French, L. (2002). *Counseling American Indians*. Boston, MA: University Press of America.

Trimble, J. (2002). Ethno-cultural considerations and strategies for providing counseling services to Native American Indians. In P. Pederson (Ed.), *Counseling across cultures*. Thousand Oaks, CA: Sage.

Herring, R. (1999). *Counseling with Native American Indians and Alaska Natives*. Thousand Oaks, CA: Sage.

Garrett, M., & Garrett, J. (1994). The path of good medicine: Understanding and counseling Native Americans. *Journal of Multicultural Counseling and Development, 22*.

Clarke, J. (1991). *A gathering of wisdoms: Tribal mental health*. Laconner, WA: Swinomish Indian Tribal Community.

Sue, S., Allen, D., & Conaway, L. (1975). The responsiveness and equality of mental health care to Chicanos and Native Americans. *American Journal of Community Psychology, 9*.

10 Hays, P. (2008) *Addressing cultural complexities in practice* (2nd ed.). Washington, DC: American Psychological Association.

Running Wolf, P., & Rickard, J. (2003) An American Indian approach to experiential learning. *Journal of Multicultural Counseling and Development, 31*.

11 Clifton, J. (1989). *Being and becoming Indian*. Chicago, IL: Dorsey.

12 Minges, P. (2004). *Black Indian slave narratives*. Winston-Salem, NC: Blair.

Brooks, J. (2002). *Confounding the color line: The Indian Black experience in North America*. Lincoln, NE: University of Nebraska Press.

Katz, W. (1997). *Black Native Americans: A hidden heritage*. New York, NY: Simon and Schuster.

Forbes, J. (1993). *Africans and Native Americans: The Language of race and the evolution of Red-Black people*. Urbana, IL: University of Illinois Press.

13 Weatherford, J. (1988). *Indian givers*. New York, NY: Faucett.

14 Clifton, J. (1989). *Being and becoming Indian*. Chicago, IL: Dorsey.

15 Utter, J. (2002). *American Indians.* Norman, OK: University of Oklahoma Press.

16 Garrotte, E. (2003). *Real Indians: Identity and the survival of Native America.* Berkeley, CA: UC Press.

Forbes, J. (1995). *Only Approved Indians.* Norman: University of Oklahoma Press.

Tiahant, M. (1993). Friends we are all Indians. In J. Gattuso (Ed.), *A circle of nations: Voices and visions of American Indians.* Hillsboro, OR: Beyond Worlds.

Wilson, T. (1992). Blood quantum: Native American mixed bloods. In M. Root (Ed.), *Racially mixed people in America.* Newbury Park, CA: Sage.

17 O'Nell, T. (1996). *Disciplined hearts: History, identity, and depression in an American Indian community.* Berkeley, CA: UC Press.

18 Fogelson, R. (1998). Perspectives on Native American identity. In R. Thornton (Ed.), *Studying Native America.* Milwaukee, WI: University of Wisconsin Press.

19 Bordewich, F. (1996). *Killing the White Man's Indian.* New York, NY: Doubleday.

20 Garrett, M., & Pichete, E. (2000). Red as an apple: Native American acculturation and counseling, with and without reservation. *Journal of Counseling and Development.*

21 Gustafson, F. (1997) *Dancing between two worlds.* Mahwah, NJ: Paulist Press

2

The Choctaw

I t is difficult to comprehend many points that Beaver makes about traditional Indian values in these interviews without some understanding of
the Choctaw people. What follows is a brief synopsis of the history, culture,
and traditional religious practices of the Choctaw. This discussion should
also help illumine the legacy of Choctaw and White relations, which were
the foundation of key challenges in Beaver's life.

Many of today's Choctaw are descendants of the great Mississippian
Mound-Building Culture that flourished along the Mississippi River from
the Great Lakes to the Gulf of Mexico from approximately the 8th century
AD to the 16th century AD. The southern part of this area is believed to
be the ancestral home of the Choctaw, Chickasaw, Creek, Seminole, and
Cherokee nations—today referred to as the "Five "Civilized" Tribes." They
were deemed "civilized" by White society because they were more open
to adopting European American cultural forms, such as developing an
alphabet. The mound builders had a hierarchal, priest-centered religion
that is related to the "sun complex" religions of the Aztecs and the Maya.
The major religious ceremony of the mound builders was the Green Corn
Ceremony, a yearly ceremony of purification, reconciliation, and renewal.
Each of the Five Tribes (Choctaw, Chickasaw, Cherokee, Creek, and Seminole) had a version of this ceremony. Traditional Choctaw still hold the
great mound at Nanih Waiya (located near the capital of the Mississippi
Band of Choctaw Indians) to be a sacred place.[1]

Choctaw tribal origin accounts state that the Choctaw and the Chickasaw traveled to Mississippi together from the west in prehistoric times,
led by two brother chiefs, Chatha and Chicksa.[2] Their languages are

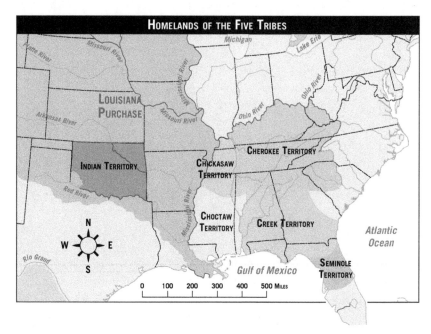

FIGURE 2.1   The "Five Civilized Tribes" before removal to the Oklahoma Indian Territory.

Source https://abagond.wordpress.com/2015/11/02/welcome-to-native-american-heritage-month-2015/

quite similar. "Chickasaw" is a Choctaw word meaning "the group that left," obviously suggesting an early split between these closely related people.

At the time of first contact with Europeans in the 16th century, there was no formal "Choctaw Nation." It was more a confederation of culturally related peoples. These people lived in a series of settlements connected by ancestry, language, and customs.[3,4] They settled (by today's map) in the southern part of Mississippi (largest group), western Alabama, northern Florida, and the northeastern corner of Louisiana. Bands of Choctaw people also lived on the grasslands west of the Mississippi River, where they competed against tribes such as the Osage in the hunt for buffalo. Sixteenth-century Choctaw were known as *pasfalaya* (long hairs) by their Chickasaw cousins because of their partial adoption of the customs of their Siouan neighbors.

In the 16th century, the Choctaw people were one of the largest, best organized, and most prosperous peoples in the Southeast. They were master farmers who produced crops in such abundance that they sold the surplus to other tribes. They produced larger yields, on smaller plots of land, than any other tribe in the region. They grew corn, potatoes, beans, melons, pumpkins, and greens. They picked fruit, nuts, and berries that grew wild. They were also renowned hunters. They hunted deer, buffalo, bear, alligator, rabbits, and birds. They fished from plentiful streams. The Choctaw were so successful at their enterprises that Choctaw became the trade language of Southeastern Indians.[5]

Like most prosperous people, the Choctaw saw war as disruptive; however, they fiercely defended themselves if attacked. I was once told by Beaver, "We are a lot like the diamondback rattlesnake. We are content to be peaceful and are tranquil if left alone, but, if you step on us, you better watch out!" Indeed, the diamondback rattlesnake is sacred to the Choctaw. Choctaw highly value practicality, self-control, honesty, integrity, generosity, and bravery in battle.

While the early Choctaw were a practical people, their lives were infused with spirituality. They believed in a Supreme Being and lesser spiritual powers. The symbol for God was the Sun, and fire was His representative on Earth. The great spiritual ceremony was the Green Corn Ceremony, which was danced around a fire. All household fires were renewed yearly from this fire. This ceremony symbolized the yearly renewal of the people. At the time of this ceremony, one was expected to forgive all wrongs—except for the murder of a relative.

Choctaw spiritual practices were in essence shamanic and geared toward helping individuals. The aim was to gain assistance and insights from powerful spirits, who revealed themselves in visions and dreams. These spirits often appeared as some aspect of the natural world. It was also believed that all plants and animals were ruled by master spirits who could be called on to produce game, cure illnesses, and offer protection from malevolent forces.

There are several Choctaw words for God, and they imply different aspects of the divine: Aba Inki ("Father Above"), Ishtahullo Chitto ("Great Sun Priest"), and Nanapesa ("Director"). Some traditional Choctaw refer to God as "the Man Above" [Beaver used this expression]. The pious Choctaw sought to stay balanced and seek order by "following the bright path that Sun has set.". To go off this path was to encounter things that are dangerous and polluting. The Circle was the symbol of the Sun (God, eternal) and the Cross the symbol of the Four Directions (Creation, everlasting). These symbols are seen on religious artifacts of the early period.[6] They are also the basis of the medicine wheel—a cross within a circle—used in Indian ceremonies in many cultures.

There were also good lesser spirits called *kwanokasha* (forest dweller) who lived in the remote parts of wooded forests. These kwanokasha had great powers and occasionally took on the task of teaching humans to be medicine persons. They were said to look like normal human beings except that they were no more than two or three feet in height.

The tools of the medicine person included herbs, medicine bags (full of sacred objects), knives for cutting, horns for sucking out poisons and witchcraft, eagle feathers, drums, and pipes. They recited prayers, sang, and danced over those in need. They conducted sweat lodges to heal and purify. They prayed to God and the four directions. In addition to the Green Corn Ceremony, there were other ceremonial dances, such as the Eagle, Buffalo, Bear, Alligator, Turkey, Snake, and War dances.

By the late 17th century, the Choctaw were continually harassed by English colonists.[7] These White men not only encroached on Choctaw land but continually raided Choctaw villages to capture slaves for Southern plantations. The English had even enlisted other Indians, mostly Chickasaw and Cherokee, as slave catchers. The Choctaw and the other tribes in the Southeast lived in terror of slave catchers, who would steal their people and force them to work on plantations. At least a thousand Choctaw were forced into Southern slavery. These captured Choctaw would eventually intermarry with African slaves on the plantations.[8] Out of desperation, the Choctaw approached the French and asked them to become allies. They obtained the guns they needed to fight against armed English slave catchers.

The Choctaw relationship with the French flourished at first. They traded furs and crops for cooking pots, guns, and horses. The Europeans soon discovered the Indian weakness for alcohol and exploited it. The Choctaw called alcohol "red water" (red was the color for hostility). Young braves got drunk and fought each other. Some Choctaw would trade a good horse for a bottle of this addictive drink. Chiefs tried to ban alcohol.

Throughout the 18th century, the Choctaw were caught up in the French wars against the English and their Indian allies (such as the Chickasaw and Cherokee). These wars drained Choctaw resources and population. By the end of the colonial period, the Choctaw had gone from a prosperous people to one that was in dire financial straits and increasingly dependent on the White society.

Things grew worse for the Choctaw after the founding of the government of the United States in 1789. European nations had related to Indians as sovereign states and potential allies. They attempted to regulate conflict between American colonists and Indians. This worked sometimes to the Indians' benefit. The new American government saw Indians as "hostiles" who needed to be civilized, removed from too close proximity to Whites, or exterminated. Indians were in the way of the westward expansion.

After the American Revolution, more Whites flooded into the Indian territory of Mississippi. They brought with them the institution of slavery from Southern states further east. They encouraged Choctaw to adopt slavery. Whites hoped that the Southern Indians would defend this evil institution if they had a stake in it. Runaway slaves often were given refuge in Indian nations. Whites also feared alliances between slaves and Indians because the two groups combined outnumbered the White population in many parts of the South.[8] In the course of time, some Southern Indians did adopt the institution of slavery. Few full bloods took slaves; most masters were White mixed bloods (Individuals of White and Indian ancestry).

The federal government repeatedly forced the Choctaw to sign a series of treaties in which they agreed to cede land. Mississippi Whites demanded that the Choctaw be removed from the state. The state government declared the Choctaw government to be under its control (in violation of the U.S. Constitution). The newly elected Mississippi congressional delegation had a friend in President Andrew Jackson and did not have to worry about the federal government overruling White interests. The federal Indian Removal Act was enacted. This law required that all Indian tribes had to be relocated west of the Mississippi River. Choctaw and other tribes such as the Cherokee were forced to leave for Oklahoma on what was termed "The Trail of Tears."

In 1830, the Choctaw were pressured to sign the Treaty of Dancing Rabbit Creek, agreeing to trade their homeland in Mississippi for new homes in what was supposed to be the "permanent" Indian territory of Oklahoma ("Oklahoma" is Choctaw for "Red People"). Chiefs were able to get the federal government to agree to allow a portion of the Choctaw people to remain on what was to be newly allocated land in Mississippi, but this promise was never kept. The common Choctaw hated the idea of removal and accused the chiefs of selling them out. Some elected Choctaw officials were recalled from office, but it was too late. Since most of the chiefs who agreed to removal were mixed-blood Christians, there were reprisals against Christian Choctaw. This conflict became a dynamic in tribal politics for years to come.

The Choctaw left for Oklahoma in the 1830s. Full bloods, mixed bloods, intermarried citizens (mostly White males), and African American slaves (many of whom were mixed with Choctaw) left for Oklahoma in the winter. This was difficult for the very young, the elderly, and the sick. Many died en route. At one point, the main group had to wade in water that was up to their waists through 30 miles of swampland in Arkansas. Those who made it to

Oklahoma were sick and/or physically exhausted. Removal also disrupted the traditional Choctaw matrilineal clan system, and the society was reorganized around local communities and a national government.

The Choctaw established farms and ranches and had 30 years of peace in Oklahoma until the coming of the Civil War. Initially, the Choctaw voted to stay neutral, but mixed blood slave owners forced a second vote. Subsequently, the Choctaw Nation joined the Confederacy, even though most full bloods wanted neutrality. At the end of the Civil War, the government of the United States punished the Choctaw for siding with the Confederacy. It gave away a large portion of Oklahoma Choctaw land to Plains Indian tribes and demanded that the Choctaw end slavery (which they did reluctantly). Although slavery had ended, Black Choctaw and Choctaw Freedmen (former African American Choctaw slaves) were not treated fairly. The Choctaw Nation allowed Whites who married Choctaw to become tribal members but outlawed marriage between Blacks and Choctaw—of course, such liaisons happened but were not officially recognized. Black Indian descendants rarely received full citizenship. Whites sometimes bribed officials to get on tribal rolls in order to get land grants. This inequity was seen throughout Southern tribes in the 19th and early 20th centuries.[9,10]

At the end of the 19th century, the Choctaw faced yet another communal defeat. In 1897, the federal government passed the General Allotment Act, also known as the Dawes Act. The purpose of this law was to impose cultural change on Indian people by ending the practice of communal land ownership. Tribal lands were subdivided and given to individual Choctaw in small parcels. After all newly enrolled individuals got their small parcels of poor-quality land, the rest was designated as "excess" and opened to White settlement. By this means, much of the Choctaw territory was lost. In 1906, the tribal government of the Oklahoma Choctaw was dissolved by federal law, although individuals still continued to receive financial resources from the federal government. There is still a Choctaw tribal government in Oklahoma today, but there is no reservation.

Life was hard for those Choctaw who remained in Mississippi. Although they had been promised land, few received it. They faced open hostility from the White population. They held an inferior status and could not even give testimony in a civil trial against a White person. Most became sharecroppers and lived in abject poverty. They tried to isolate themselves as much as they could from the hostile White community. They were constantly urged by the Bureau of Indian Affairs to give up their claims to Mississippi land and move to Oklahoma, and this went on until the beginning of the 20th century. The last large migration of Mississippi Choctaw left for Oklahoma around 1910; still, some remained in Mississippi.

The federal government finally relented and set up a Choctaw Indian agency in Mississippi in 1918, and a reservation was approved in 1934. Because of strong tribal leadership and tribally owned businesses, it has become one of the most prosperous Indian reservations in the United States. They reflect the old Choctaw ingenuity and practicality in adapting to changing circumstances without losing their essential Indian ways.

Today, Choctaw are the third-largest tribe of American Indians. They are spread across four different "recognized" Indian nations: the Mississippi Band of Choctaw (federally recognized), located in Neshoba ("wolf") County in Mississippi, with a enrolled population of about 10,000; the Choctaw Nation of Oklahoma (federally recognized), whose capital is in Tuskahoma ("red warrior"), Oklahoma, with an enrolled population of about 250,000; the Jena Band of Choctaw, located near Creola, Louisiana, with a enrolled population of about 1,000; and the Mowa Choctaw (state recognized), located near the banks of the Mobile and Tombigbee Rivers in Alabama, with an enrollment of about 6,000. Modern-day Choctaw speak Choctaw and/or English. While some participate in the traditional tribal religion, most are Christian.

Notes

1 Thomas, D. (1993). Indian Confederacies. In M. Reagen (Ed.), *The Native Americans*. Atlanta, GA: Turner Publishing.

2 Swanton, J. (2001). *Source material for the social and ceremonial life of the Choctaw Indians*. [Original publication date 1931 as a Bulletin of The Smithsonian Institution]. Tuscaloosa, AL: University of Alabama Press.

3 Carson, J. (1999). *Searching for the bright path: The Mississippi Choctaw from prehistory to removal*. Lincoln, NE: University of Nebraska Press.

4 McKee, J. (1989). *The Choctaw*. New York, NY: Chelsea House.

5 Reeves, C. (1985) *The Choctaw before removal*. Jackson, MS: University of Mississippi Press.

6 Carson, op. cit.

7 Wright, J. (1990). *The only land they knew: The world of the Southern Indians*. New York, NY: Collier.

8 Katz, W. (1986). *Black Indians*. New York, NY: Aladdin.

9 Brooks, J. (2002). *The Indian-Black experience in North America.* Lincoln, NE: University of Nebraska Press.

10 Forbes, J. (1990). The manipulation of race, caste, and identity: Classifying Afro Americans, Native Americans and Red-Black people. *Journal of Ethnic Studies, 17* (4), 24.

3

Growing Up as a Traditional Choctaw—The Importance of Community

During my interview with Beaver, I asked him to describe his early upbringing in the Choctaw Nation of Oklahoma, and we had an in-depth conversation during which he touched upon many important issues. He extolled the communal social customs of the Choctaw people and the great value placed on generosity. He described a loving family environment and the tragic death of his mother when he was a young child. Beaver offered colorful accounts of the activities of his great-uncle (who was a medicine man) and the ways in which he was a positive role model of Choctaw values. He also discussed the deep division that existed among the Choctaw who, like his family, tried to adhere to Choctaw cultural values (traditionals) and those who wanted to assimilate more completely to Euro American ways (progressives).

Another theme was Choctaw intermarriage with other peoples. Beaver said that non-Choctaw were treated no differently than tribal members in his community; however, he described troubled relationships between mixed blood and full blood Choctaw. He criticized the efforts of the federal government to force cultural assimilation on the Choctaw. He argued that the federal policies of allotment and enrollment have been divisive issues for Indian people. He urged Indian people to be more tolerant. He urged modern day Choctaw to return to their traditional values.

Beaver:

My name is Turner Arthur Berry, Jr. I am named after my father. My dad started calling me Beaver long before I could remember. I thought that was my name for a long time. I didn't know that I had another name. If anybody asked me, "What's your name?" I'd say, "Beaver." I thought that was my name. They called me Beaver because I was always on the go, busy doing something.

I was born April 2, 1923, in Monroe, Oklahoma, in the Choctaw Nation. The Choctaw have been there for a while. My great uncle, grandpa, mom, and dad were born in Oklahoma Indian Territory. I was raised seven miles south of Wilburton, Oklahoma. Wilburton is near McAlister, Oklahoma. Back then, there were a lot of wild hogs and bears. It was wild country, a mountain area. Our community was out in the woods. It was a mixed community, but mostly Choctaw Indian people. My mother's name was Mary Jane Collins. I had two sisters and two brothers. The youngest brother passed away when he was a baby. I was the second child.

When I was a boy, a lot of Choctaw would get together and do their ceremonies. We would have Green Corn Dances and play stickball and things like that. Tribal gatherings and ceremonies occurred mostly around the turn of spring, summer, fall, and winter. When I was a small kid, there were a lot of small kids to play with, and to me it was fun time. There was always a big feast. Eating time and fun time. A lot of playing, a lot of interaction with other kids. One thing about the Choctaw people: you didn't have to worry about your kids because there would be somebody who would make sure they were all right. If an adult saw somebody's kid about to get into something he shouldn't be doing, they would correct that kid. That was permissible to Choctaw people. You could correct any child in the tribe; you did not have to be a close relative. The Choctaw people were one big family. We all pulled together. Back then, they didn't sell nothin'. All the food was free, and you ate anytime you wanted to. When you got hungry, you went to see what was cooking and could get something to eat. Women, elderly ladies, would be there all day serving and cooking. We shared as a community. Everybody just shared what they had.

If you were a widow woman or widower, somebody was always coming by seeing about you, even if you lived alone. You were never totally forgotten.

Somebody always came to see if you needed something or wanted something done. You belonged to that community. Everybody in that community looked after one another. When I was growin' up back there in Oklahoma, you never locked your door. Your door was always open, and if somebody come by and was hungry, and if they wanted to eat, they'd go in and eat what was there. Generally they'd write a note and say, "I was

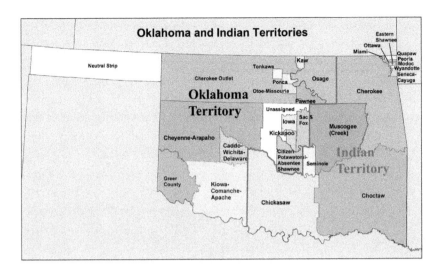

FIGURE 3.1 Oklahoma Indian Territory in 19th Century.

here, and no one was here, and I came in to eat." If they needed a coat, and they seen one hanging up on the wall, it was for them to take. If they needed it, they would take it. If they didn't need it, they wouldn't take it. That was kinda the custom back then.

We looked after people. There was this old lady, she lived down the road from us. Every time we'd go by there, my dad would stop and make sure that she was okay. Nearest spring was half a mile away; we carried our drinking water from the spring. He'd make sure that she had plenty of water and wood—in the wintertime, he'd make sure she had wood. During the summertime, he made sure she had plenty drinking water. Whatever her needs might be, and she wasn't no relation of ours. Matter fact, she was a White woman, but she was a human bein'. The first thing, she was a human bein', and the community accepted her that way. If you're human, as long as you're here in this community, we're gonna help you fulfill whatever your needs might be. I was raised up with those kind of values. That's the Indian way.

It wasn't just Indian people in the community. There were Black people, White people, and Mexican people, but it was mostly Choctaw. There was a lot of coal minin' in Oklahoma. That's where you got a lot of other races of people come in to mine coal. That's when Mexicans come in.

The Choctaw people mixed and married with other people. They had mixed blood Choctaw. My dad's a half breed. My mother's a full blood

Choctaw. Some of the full bloods didn't like the half breeds. Some of the half breeds didn't like the full bloods. I used to hear it from both sides of the family—on my mother's side and my daddy's side. The mixed bloods used to say, "Don't be hard-headed. Don't grow up and be hard-headed like those full bloods." The full bloods would tell me, "Don't grow up and be stupid and ignorant like those half breeds." You did have a conflict over values. Most of your full bloods followed "traditional" Choctaw ways. Most mixed breeds were more "progressive" in that they wanted to adopt more of the White ways. I am three quarters Choctaw and one quarter Irish.

We also had a lot of Black and Choctaw mixtures in our community. There were probably more Black mixed-blood Choctaw than White mixed-blood Choctaw. The only way you could tell the difference between a Black Choctaw and an African American would be by the way they acted. Not by the way the tribe treated 'em or anything like that. Sometimes you couldn't even tell whether they was mixed or not cuz they didn't show Black or they didn't show too much Indian. If they was Indian and African, you couldn't tell by their appearance what side they was gonna identify with more.

You can't tell by looking how much Indian a person is. I got a sister, and she's got two daughters. One of 'em—and they both got the same daddy—one of 'em looks like a full blood Choctaw. Other looks like she ain't got a drop. A person might have Indian blood, but they might not show it. You had your White mixed bloods and your Black mixed bloods, but we all functioned as a group.

There was some prejudice—for example, with kids. If you're quarter breed, or you look more White than you do Indian, and you're playin' with some fuller bloods, (and you got some dark people in that mixture), they'll holler, "Don't give the ball to that White boy. Give it to one of us." They was talkin' that way about kids on their own team! Now this actually happened with a high school basketball team. When I was a boy, the full bloods would say, "The half breeds are the people who are gonna get us into trouble." I don't think the quantum of blood makes you Indian. I've seen some quarter breeds. Matter of fact, I've seen some White folks who was raised around the Choctaw Nation, and they had the same value system. They was more Indian, more Choctaw, than a lot of the full-bloods were. Being Indian is more about culture than race.

There is also a problem with using tribal enrollment, as opposed to a person knowin' their Indian culture, as a way of deciding who is Indian, because some tribes didn't have relationships with the United States government. It is like with that story you showed me about that Indian basketball league. Some boys came down to the Southwest from up North. They were playin' a team down in Arizona, most of whom were dark skinned; many of the ones from the northern place had very fair complexions. Anyway, these teams got into a dispute. I think the southern dark skinned team was winning. The northern team demanded to see the other team's C.D.I.B. (Certificate of Degree of Indian Blood) cards, because they thought they were really Mexicans. This is strange to me, because most Mexicans have Indian blood. It got to be a big controversy, and some of the southern ones said, "We come from tribes, some of us, that don't have treaties with the American government. We don't have cards because we've never had a political relationship with the United States. Our tribes are in Mexico. Our people came from there." The officials disqualified the southwestern team because some of their guys didn't have CDIB cards. The officials said, "Only _real_ Indians can play in the U.S.A."[1] That was wrong. We were Indians long before there were U.S. government officials.

I don't think Indian people should focus too much on whether you're a half breed or whether you're full blood, or whether you're one or three quarters or whether you are enrolled or not. To me, I've met people from across the border with Mexican Indian ancestry. I think it's up to that individual to say whether he's Indian or not. Many Mexicans are a lot more Indian than Spanish. If they say they're Indians, I think they should be treated as such. See, back when the White man came over, we didn't have no boundaries from Canada all the way down to Mexico. Indians roamed. They traveled a lot. A lot of 'em intermarried with other tribes. I have seen some Indians reject other Indians because they were from Mexico. I think that stinks!

You take a prejudiced person, they'll find those prejudiced things to say about other people. A good example of this—a few years ago in San Francisco I heard about this other controversy. There was going to be a Native American Culture day, and there was a big division because some groups wanted to allow the Mexican Indians to have a booth, but other Indian people insisted they couldn't be a part of it, because Mexican Indians didn't have a relationship with the American government through treaty. The upshot is that the Mexican Indians did not get a booth. The people who discriminated against those Mexican Indians were trying to feel special at someone else's expense.

If Indians want to practice their Indian culture, even if it comes from old Mexico, I think they should feel free to do so and should be recognized as Indians and be accepted, not only by the Indian community but by all communities anywhere they go in this United States. If a person comes to me and says, "I'm a Indian," I take him at face value. I don't ask him for a C.D.I.B card or say, "Show me a card." I don't ask him anything like that.

To me, a CDIB card is not goin' to make you no more Indian than what you are. It's just proof that you have Indian ancestors. It's just documentation. It doesn't say how traditional you are. You could be documented and be totally Whitewashed. Even if a person has only one drop of Indian blood in him and he wants to honor it by learning Indian ways, that is his right.

Let me say more about my family life when I was a boy. If we went to town, we went once or twice a year. We would load up the wagon. We'd all go in the wagon. Indians like to do things together. You would see dogs following behind the wagons. We were in real rural country—country living, but also group living, too. Elders would get together and talk a lot.

I was 12 years old when my mother passed. She was 32 years old when she died. I guess back then 32 years of age for Indian people was kinda considered old. She died of TB. She had been sick about a year, and the doctor gave her some medicine, but back then the doctors didn't know too much, and the medicine did no good. My mother's mother took my two sisters to her place, and my great-uncle took me and my brother and my dad. He was my mama's uncle, part of her clan. It would be more likely that the mother's relatives would take you in among the Choctaw.

My uncle's name was Sim Collins. The people who lived around there were afraid of him. They called him a witch doctor. He wasn't a witch doctor. He was a medicine man. He was very much a spiritual human being. He believed in the Creator as he understood Him. If he had anything and you needed it, he would just give it to you. If you needed a place to live, he'd say, "Go back there and build you a log cabin." He wouldn't charge you anything for it. He tried to help people any way he could. I picked up a lot of values from my great uncle. Made me what I am today.

I never remember a time of settin' down at a table with just my great aunt and my great uncle, just immediate family being there. There would always be total strangers sitting at that table. We had a long table. Anybody come there, the first thing you did was feed 'em. You didn't ask 'em if they was hungry or if they needed to eat or wanted to eat. My great aunt would supply the meal. Even total strangers were coming there, 'cuz you know how the word gets around. "If you're hungry, go to uncle Sim's. He's got food. If you need a place to build that log cabin, go to Uncle Sim. He's got land; he's got that Indian allotment. He'll give you some land, and you can build a cabin."

My uncle was a very honest man. His handshake was better than a signed contract. The White bankers knew that and would loan him money on a verbal commitment and a handshake. Generous people like my uncle more or less kept the community together. They had respect from a lot of people. Still, regardless of how good you get or how good you are to other people, there will be some people in a community who will dislike you for reasons of their own. You don't always know who it is or their reasons, but you will find those kinds of people in a community, both with the Indians and with the non-Indians. You'll always find negative people. Any community you go into, you'll find negative people.

My uncle was around all my childhood. He was running sweats. He was a medicine man. He did pipe ceremonies and things like that. I saw him do many things. He used a stone pipe and a wooden pipe and a pipe made out of a corncob on a long stem. They'd come to him for practically everything.

Sometimes a horse would get lost, and they asked my uncle, "Where would be the best place to find that horse?" He'd tell them, and they'd find the horse. Me and my uncle would run wild horses out of mountains and corral them. He'd see one and want to break it. He broke it and put the saddle on it. He would jerk a hair from behind the wild horse's ear and put it in my shirt pocket. He said, "When you get through riding this horse, look for this hair in your pocket." I would get on and ride and break that horse, and I'd get off and look for that hair. I could never find that hair. We used to go catch wild horses. My uncle would circle a group of wild horses while spreading medicine on the ground, singing as he rode. Then he would point to the lead horse and show him the direction he wanted him to lead the herd, and they would follow. Very few people who were present could believe what they saw him do. I was amazed. It blew me out.

By the time I was about 15, 16 years old, I thought I was a good rider. The community also thought I was a pretty good rider, and they entered me in the Indian rodeo at Wilburton. My uncle said, "I am not going to go to the rodeo and watch you, because you can't ride. My medicine helped you break those horses in the past." I did not believe him. However, first horse I rode threw me high as a kite. I came back, and I told my uncle.

FIGURE 3.2 **The Lakota Medicine Man Slow Bull.**

Edward S. Curtis, http://www.sonofthesouth.net/union-generals/sioux-indians/sioux-indians.htm.

He said, "How did you do?" I said, "Not too good." He said, "I knew it. I told you, you can't ride." He was good at things like that.

I knew he could do these things, so one time I asked him to teach me, 'cuz there were a bunch of young girls I wanted to date, and there were some boys I wanted to put some medicine down on. I said, "Teach me to do these things." He told me, "Your heart is in the wrong place. I'm not going to tell you nuthin'."

My uncle was a good healer. I had a fight with a White man. The White man shot me in my arm. The doctors said all the muscles were destroyed. The doctors said they couldn't fix it. Doctors said the only thing that arm would be good for was to fill a shirtsleeve. I couldn't use the arm. For a long time I picked it up, moved it around, but I didn't have control over it. My uncle asked me, "You want to stay a cripple the rest of your life?" I said, "No." "Want to do something about it?" I said, "Yeah." He said, "Okay, I'll doctor you. I'm going to tell you what you have to do to get using that arm again." He said, "Every day, you take your hand and work your fingers like that. You do that every day and use the medicine I'm giving you." He said, "Go ahead and do it. It's going to hurt you. Move those fingers now. You got to get where you can move that arm." I kept working with it. It hurt. I kept taking that medicine he had given me. I raised it up. It got to where I could use it. When I went back to the doctors, they were amazed: "You're not supposed to have muscles. How'd you do it?" I said, "I don't know. You're the doctor. You tell me." He said, "Those muscles are healing themselves; they're healing back together." I didn't tell them about my uncle. My uncle told me not to. They wouldn't believe it anyway.

A lot of the White people in our community, even the woman I married and her people, to this day say my great uncle was a witch doctor. They didn't believe in the Indian ways. My daughter, oldest daughter, _she_ believes her great great uncle was a witch doctor. She asked me about it one time, and I had to explain to her he wasn't a witch doctor, not like her mama and grandma told her. He did not do evil things.

My uncle told me one time how he became a medicine man, that he was taken away by kwanokasha and taught. Before he came back, they taught him all these things. I guess he was a little guy when this happened. He spent most of his life as a medicine man. I grew up attending his sweat ceremonies since I was a little guy. They felt good. He was real traditional, but I think all his medicine and all his healing, all those other things came directly from the spirits. He told me, "If you ever start the spiritual way, don't use that altar for anything but for helping people. The same altar can be used for good or for bad. If you cross that line to the bad, you'll never get back over here to the good."

If you come to him for very specific doctoring, he would sit you down and have a ceremony. Most would bring him tobacco. Then they'd sit down and have a ceremony. He knew herbs and medicines. Whatever was wrong with you, he would see it within you, and he'd know what herb to give you. He said, "What I know, the little people [kwanokasha] give me."[2]

He could even predict the future and tell the outcome of certain events. Before I went to World War II, I went down to see him. He had a log under a tree. We'd go sit on that log. I don't know what that log had to do with it, but that was his place. He went there to counsel/doctor people. Before I went off to the service in WWII, he took me to the log and he said, "You are going away, going to the war, but you are going to make it back okay. You are going to come back a hero. You ain't going to get killed." A lot of times I thought that old Indian didn't know what he was talking about. I was in some tight spots in the Pacific. I saw people killed around me daily, but I did get the Silver Star.

He was the only one in our local community who worked with the spirit helpers. There was another man. He was Choctaw and Black. He healed with herbs. You'll find most medicine people are one way or the other: they either rely on spirits or they work with herbs. Some can use both. He helped a lot of people, but my uncle always told me, "Look in their eyes, and if they give you a creepy feeling, get away from them." People come through and some of them bewitched the people. My uncle told me about one who was a witch. He stopped those people when they came around.

My uncle was my greatest teacher. He said, "What I'm doing today, the Creator will one day give to you." I haven't got there yet. I know the Creator had to be with him. He was a true medicine man. I can't do the things I seen him do. My uncle died 30 years ago. In the Indian community, some of them really lost it when he died; however, the White community seemed like they were kind of glad. They thought, "Well, that old witch is gone." The White folks were really scared of him. He never used his powers against the White community. They just knew what he could do. Most of those old time (traditional) Choctaws had faith in my uncle. There were a lot of other Choctaws, however, who had adopted White ways (progressive).

My dad was a spiritual man as well. He said when all Indian people create a circle and get together in the circle, they will have everything back they lost. They would get their land back, everything. I said, "Why not get all the Choctaw people together and make that circle?" Now I know what he meant. When all the tribes get together, put away the politics and animosity, the Creator will give us back what we lost. My father practiced what he preached. My family was very loving, very close.

My great grandmother was born in Mississippi. She told us that the Choctaw were a prosperous people when they left Mississippi. They had plantations and farms and a lot of things that were valuable. When they come to Oklahoma, that was all taken away from them. Removal didn't leave them anything. They became like beggars. They had to become one of the "good old boys" in order to get what they needed to survive and to save their kids. They figured the best route to survival was to conform to the White community. A lot of Choctaw passed themselves off as Whites. They did that so they could get jobs. In the process, they conformed, and their kids conformed. They ended up more White than Choctaw.

There are still a few traditional Choctaw in Oklahoma, but they don't advertise themselves. You have to hunt them out. They see things the same as I do. When I was young, there was conflict between what we called "progressives" who wanted to adopt White ways and the "traditionals" who wanted to stick to the old Choctaw ways. You had two factions in the Indian world, the Choctaw world—the progressives and the traditionals. They would argue about what's traditional and what's not traditional. How you do things and how you don't do things. "These are not our ways. This [Christianity] is not our church." The traditionals didn't believe in the U.S. Federal Government. They looked at the White man as trying to get over on them. That's why you have a lot of Choctaw today not enrolled. Some don't have roll numbers. They were afraid that the government would take their names and do them in again. They wouldn't register because they were afraid it would somehow be used against them. You have a lot of Choctaw in Oklahoma that are Choctaw but can't prove it according to the government, because they have no roll numbers. We lost a lot of land.

My dad said this about allotment and enrollment: "The federal government is doing us like we do chickens." He told me, "Go get me some corn, and I'll show you." I went to get him an ear of corn. He started to shell out some corn, and he put some down around by our feet, and he said, "Now which chicken do you want?" I said, "That one right there." He threw more corn down in front of that chicken, and when it came around that corn, my dad reached down and picked that chicken up. "That's what the federal government is doing to us with this allotment and enrollment." He said the federal government does the same thing to us Indian people. They give us just enough to start fighting and squabbling over and then pick us off one at a time. I see that squabbling in our Indian societies today.

I really feel enrollment is an injustice to an Indian person. We're the only race of people that has to prove who we are. No other group of people has to prove that. So therefore, it's an injustice. If everybody had to prove and carry cards about who they are and what their ancestors were, then I couldn't say it's an injustice. No one else has to prove anything. So to me, if this White man had to prove that he was White, a Jew had to prove that he was a Jew, this Mexican had to prove that he was Mexican, these African Americans had to prove that they was African Americans, and all these other races had to prove who they were and what they were, then I couldn't sit here and say that's an injustice. When you pick out one certain people and say you have to prove who you are, then to me that's an injustice. I don't accept this U.S. government as my government. It belongs to the White folks.

These blood quantum issues are still havin' an impact on people like my grandson. He's going to college. He's proud to be who he is and what he is, but slowly they're taking that away from him because he looks White. They ask him if he's really Indian. This embarrasses a person. It hurts the Indian people as a whole. It's a negative process, and anytime you get into negativity it has negative impact on other individuals. You hear this all the time. With Indian people, they'll ask you a lotta times when they get mad at 'ya, "I've gotta CDIB card. Have you got one?" in a derogatory manner. It's not in a good way. If you don't have a CDIB card, a lot of these Indian organizations, they won't even consider you Indian. If you don't look Indian and there is a difference of opinion, you sure better have that CDIB card!

I refused to get officially enrolled for most of my life even though I am three quarters Choctaw and both my parents were enrolled. I only enrolled later in life so my kids and grandkids could get help if they needed it. Today, if you got a roll number, you're entitled to scholarships, to fundin' for education, for higher education. Things like that. If you don't have a roll number, even if everybody knows that you're Indian, that probably won't count.

The way that the system is now, it's no good. Maybe one tribe will accept a more lenient standard for membership and another tribe is more strict. I am not sure what the solution is, but I do know that we have to make room for the nonenrolled Indians while being on guard against those who say they are Indian only to get a financial benefit.

Still, the government has also used benefits to control Indians. That's not a new thing with the federal government. They used the reservations to keep the Indians at bay. They used the BIA to ration out the food. If you was on a war party, they'd say, "Well, you don't get nothin' this month because you went off, you went out on a raid." Maybe you had some children at home. Instead of you bein' the one that suffered, mainly, your kids suffered. They knew how to control that man.

I like to see traditional Indians. If I see Indians acting too much like they are White folks, I get upset. I see it now as, unfortunately, few still believe in the traditional ways of their people. What made it harder for my uncle than it does for me, having lived so many years in California—his own people, the Choctaw, were against him. So many of them were giving up our traditions. Progressives didn't like my uncle. When they talked about him, they always had bad things to say about him. In those days, they had violence between the traditionals and the progressives. The traditionals wanted the Choctaw to stay as they were when they lived in Mississippi. The progressives wanted to lean more towards the White way. By the time I was growing up, it was more verbal arguments.

You are likely to see social dances today among the Choctaw. My great niece married a Cherokee. My nephew's uncle was keeper of the stomp dance. He is very traditional. The only way you could get into this dance is by invitation. They have kept a ceremonial fire going ever since they come to Oklahoma. We Choctaw also had the stomp dance. We practice the stomp dance in California at California Choctaw gatherings. I mostly go to the Cherokee stomp dance these days.

Notes

1   Forbes, J. (1995). *Only approved Indians can play in the U.S.A.* Norman, OK: University of Oklahoma Press.
2   Carson, J. (1999). op., cit

4

At War With the World

In the upcoming pages, Beaver recounts his childhood experiences in an abusive Indian boarding school where Indian children were taught to devalue their Indian culture and heritage. He describes the resultant sadness, anger, and confusion boarding school induced in him and other Indian children. He could no longer receive solace from the spiritual teachings of his medicine man uncle or loving Choctaw community.

The Indian boarding schools were started in the mid-19th century and continued in great force through most of the 20th century. There was no real check on them until the passage of the Indian Child Welfare Act in 1978, which returned control of Indian children to their families, tribes, and the Indian community. The stated goal of these schools was to assimilate American Indians into mainstream American culture. Their slogan was "Kill the Indian and save the man." The ethnocentric Whites who led this movement were actually in the more liberal wing of Indian policy in the 19th century. Their stated goal was to essentially turn Indians into brown-skinned Euro Americans. Other extreme right-wing genocidal factions argued for the total elimination of Indians: "The only good Indian is a dead Indian." Either way, both groups envisioned a "vanishing Indian" who would ultimately disappear from American life.

The proponents of the Indian boarding schools thought the best way for Indian tribes to become assimilated was to indoctrinate Indian children. The hope was that these children would integrate into American society and take Christian Euro American cultural values back to their tribal communities. Their cruel approach involved forcefully removing children from loving families and placing them in cold residential schools far from home—making future contact with the family difficult at best. Upon arriving at these schools, the children were told that their cultures were backward and stupid. They were told that their Native religions were evil and henceforth they would practice Christianity. Children were forced to dress in the fashion of Whites of the time, and they were required to cut their hair (which was traumatizing to some from tribes who believed their soul flowed through their hair). Children who continued to speak their tribal languages often had their mouths washed out with soap. They were all forced to forget their tribal names and take English names. Children had to march about in military fashion, wear uniforms, and do menial labor for nearby Whites. Many of their White caretakers were harsh disciplinarians. Psychological, physical, and sexual abuse was also commonplace. Some of the institutions were quite unsanitary. Life-threatening epidemics of diseases such as TB were common. Indian parents feared for the health of their children, as these institutions became known as places were children often died.

This attempt to socialize these children and their tribes was a failure. When Indian children finally returned home, they no longer fit into their communities. They often had confused ethnic identities—neither White nor Indian. They had not had parental role models, so they did not know how to be marital partners and parents. This sometimes led to spousal and child abuse/neglect. Many were angry, anxious, and depressed. They turned to drugs and alcohol to soothe themselves. This led to an epidemic of substance abuse and concomitant behavior such as suicide and automobile accidents. Their marginal education in boarding school did not properly prepare them for the work world, so many led a life of poverty. For more information about the Indian boarding schools and concomitant trauma, see the references at the end of this chapter.

Below, Beaver also discusses becoming a marine in World War II after leaving boarding school. Beaver finds comfort in joining the Marine Corps, as he no longer has to figure things out—whether the White way or Indian way is better. He only has to stay alive. In spite of becoming a decorated war hero, after his discharge, Beaver is an angrier, sadder, and more confused person. He is racked with remorse over the killing he had to do in the war. After his discharge, he develops a serious drinking problem, which gets worse after his wife of 11 years takes his beloved children and runs away without a word about where the family went. He continues to spiral down into a life of chronic alcoholism, impulsive behavior, and crime. Fortunately, he makes a decision to change his life for the better in his early 40s.

Beaver:

A year after my mother died, I went off to Indian boarding school, Jones Academy. I was about 13 years old. From then on, I saw my family only when school was out during the summer months. The school was about 40 miles away, but that was a long distance back then. The kids there didn't get to see their parents much during the school year. A White guy ran Jones Academy. The staff was all White except an assistant who was Choctaw. Those White people decided that they wanted to turn us into brown-skinned White people.

The families did not protest when they came to take you to boarding school. They knew it was no good to say anything. They just come and got you. They'd take you to Indian school and teach you the "American way." The Whites felt we Indians had to conform faster. The government thought they knew better. The difference between home and boarding school was like daylight and dark. All the traditional things I'd done with my great-uncle, the boarding school didn't like. You couldn't talk your language. You couldn't talk Choctaw. We didn't go to stomp dances or anything like that.

We were forced to go to church. You wore a suit and a tie on a Sunday because we had to go to Sunday school. Boarding schools were more into the punishment-type things than we were. Indians are more or less into shaming you. If you do something wrong, they make you feel bad about it. They would shame you. In the boarding school, their theory was "punish that bad Indian." In order to keep from getting punished, you try to do what your supervisors are suggesting that you do. You kind of played along. Maybe you didn't like it. Maybe you really wasn't believin' what they was tellin' you, but you just done it.

They told us that the Choctaw way is no good: "You're a heathen. We're going to teach you the Christian way, that's God's way." They lined all the guys up, and they had to go to church. If you didn't do as told, you was gonna get punished. The physical punishment was they'd line everybody up along the sidewalk at Jones Academy, maybe two or three hundred students there, and give 'em all a belt. The boy to be punished had to run past everyone, and that's what they called "runnin' 'em through the belt line." If you didn't hit that person (if he's your friend and you didn't want to hit 'em) or hit him hard enough, then they'd run *you* through. This had a bad effect on lots of people.

Most of the Indian kids who went to the boarding schools come out—I know I did—with anger towards the White race of people. To me, and I know to a lot of Indian guys that went to Jones Academy, they generalized in the same terms. The only ones that really didn't was those that today we refer to as "apples"—they're Red on the outside and White on the inside. They tried to become White. I can't say the boarding schools are all bad. I guess if you really want to learn how to become a White person, and give up your principles and your Indian values, that's the place to go. I wouldn't send a dog to an Indian school. Now, that there is my opinion. It wouldn't have been so bad if they didn't try to make you give up everything that you valued and make you something that you wasn't.

They also had a way of lettin' you know that you ought to be thankful, appreciate them, because they was tryin' to teach you a good way. They was tryin' to teach you how to be "civilized." You were supposed to be thankful that they was there to take their time to try to help that poor, dumb Indian. Even to this day, when I think about those teachers and the boarding schools and the way they were and the way they functioned, I still get angry. I don't think the boarding school has done the Indian—the Choctaw people—any good. I think they've taken away more than they given.

Life in the boarding school was tough. We were a bunch of sad kids. We didn't do too good, because the teachers there didn't give us anything, any goals. The best you could look forward to was being a farmer or house painter or something like that. If you was a good football player or track man, good boxer, good basketball player, you was seen as a pretty good kid, but if you wasn't, they treated you pretty bad. It was pretty rough, especially if you got caught talking your language. They'd run you through the belt line. Most of us knew that the staff and faculty didn't particularly care about us. They looked like they were there for the job and to make money, that kind of situation.

The staff really confused us. They'd say, "Your religion is all heathenism. That's wrong. We're going to teach you different. We're going to teach you the right way, the Christian way." I'd go back and tell my uncle, "You told me wrong," and he'd say, "They're telling you wrong." I got to the point I didn't believe him or believe them. What they really done is take away my belief system. I didn't believe nobody. I didn't believe what my uncle was telling me. I didn't believe what they was telling me. I was out in limbo.

I questioned what I'd seen my uncle do. I became more in doubt of doing things that way. Things got a little shadier. I doubted I had really seen all that medicine. You begin to think, "Did I really see that, or am I just thinking it up?"

I started to feel kind of odd at home. After being gone, you lose a lot of communication. When I was a little guy growing up, we had good communication. While I was away from home, I listened to these people tell me what's wrong with the Indian lifestyle. You kind of lose your trust, self-respect, and your respect for other Indians. I ended up believing in nothing.

I knew if you adopt the White man's way you end up abusing the Indian people, especially other Choctaw. I would say that the only time I had contact with Indian values was during the summer. The rest of the year, I was with those teachers and instructors at the Jones Academy and got away from true Indian values. There was no argument; the students had no voice, no legal recourse. You were at the mercy of these White people who saw you as backward.

The overall effect of being in the boarding school is that I got meaner. I started to look at White people in a negative way. I think that had a lot of influence on how I feel today about White folks. I have individual White friends, but I do not trust the White society. At Jones, I would get into more fights with the White boys around the community. On the weekends, we used to go looking for White boys to beat up. Only things left was having a good time and fighting.

When I left the boarding school, I was caught between two beliefs: the White way and the Choctaw traditional way. Then I got in the Marine Corps. The only thing that they was interested in was teaching you how to fight, get drunk, and chase wild women. I was thinkin', "I have found heaven." Fight, get drunk, and chase women—and I done my share of it. I liked that. I had a lot of anger in me, so fighting just came natural. I didn't have to figure things out anymore. I even became a professional boxer. In the Marine Corps, they really didn't care if you believed in anything. Only thing they wanted to do was teach you how to kill people. I thought, "This is where I belong."

I was in World War II. I was on Guadalcanal. I was in British Samoa. I was on American Samoa. I was in the Marshall Islands. I was in the Hawaiian Islands. I did invasion on Guam. I did invasion on the Marshalls. We was on the island right off of Guadalcanal, and we went to five or six other islands. We was island-hopping.

Indians were observers. We called down fire, artillery fire, or we called in airplanes to come in and dive-bomb. Many Indians in the service were put in scouting positions. I was in the tank battalion—I was radioman in a tank. The orders came down that they had openings for all Indians to become forward observers, or scout snipers. That was sent out to all stateside headquarters. My captain got a memorandum to that effect. There was two of us in there, in our tank corps, in that particular tank battalion. We were Indians, and the first sergeant called us and said, "This is a volunteer job." We could become forward observers. He said, "It's best if you accept this offer." It was supposed to have been on a volunteer basis, but it was kinda if you don't volunteer, things was gonna be pretty rough for you. It wasn't said in that manner, but we got the message. So he and I bargained. We wanted to go to Tijuana for a weekend. We bargained with the first sergeant. We said, "If you give us a weekend pass to Tijuana, we'll volunteer." We was here stateside then. We was takin' our trainin' here in California. When we shipped out from here, we was already forward observers.

When we was on Guam, we made the initial beachhead, and we was goin' forward. We was forward recon. My forward observer officer's rifle jammed. He had one of those little carbon .30–30s, and I told him, "Throw that damn thing away. It's gonna get you killed." He threw it away. I told him, "You can pick up one. There's all kinds of weapons laying around here with these guys gettin' killed." I said, "They won't need 'em. Just get you one." He threw his away, and we started advancing forward.

We walked about a hundred yards, and this Japanese soldier jumped out and was chargin' him with a bayonet. I was carrying a Thompson submachine gun. It uses .45c ammo. At a distance of about 10 or 15 yards from where he was at, I opened fire on him and cut him about half in two with that submachine gun. During that same day, we was gettin' heavy artillery fire from the Japanese forces, and one of our forward observer members got wounded over the front line. I went out and brought him back to the front line. With killing that Japanese, and going up there and gettin' that friend of ours, our teammate, they awarded me the Silver Star. My uncle predicted that one before I left. He didn't say the Silver Star—he said, "You gonna get a medal."

I still have dreams over that one. See, with us, in the way I was taught and the way I was raised, you don't take something that you cannot give back. I had taken that Japanese soldier's life, and there's no way I can restore life to him again. Now I have these dreams. I have these bad feelins' about takin' that person's life. I feel so strongly 'bout not taking another person's life that I'm against the death penalty. I even opposed the death penalty for a man who killed one of my sons. I don't care what the circumstances are. I've talked to a lot of people about the way I feel, and they said, "That was in a time of war, and you was fightin' for your country." To me, there's got to be a better solution other than killin' another human bein' and calling it war. That's our politicians' way of sayin' it's okay to kill somebody.

I feel it's wrong to kill people, regardless of what they say or how they say it. To me, there's only one person has the right to call you to say, "It's over. It's done. Come home." That's God himself. I'm not God. I'm just tryin' to be the servant of the Creator. When you kill someone, that stays with you. Until this day, it's on my mind. When I go to sleep at night, I dream about it. I still have those dreams. It won't go away. It's not like a sore toe that will get well. I blame the government for making me kill that Japanese guy that didn't do anything to me. I talked to a lot of people about it. They say, "He would have killed you," but it still don't make it right. I might have drank a little before I went into the Marine Corps, but I started drinking heavy after I got in the Marine Corps.

I asked a lot of Indian guys when I went into combat, "What are we fighting for?" They said, "The land." None would say, "For the government." To this day, I do not claim the U.S. government as my government. I am a citizen of the Choctaw Nation. I fought to protect the land.

The impact on me of being in the war was negative. I got more aggressive. Always fighting and drinking. I got in trouble with the law and got in a lot of trouble with White folks back in Oklahoma after I got home. Sometimes I used to fight with good friends just for fun. We would get drunk and go back to being bosom buddies after throwing punches. My sisters used to be scared we were going to kill ourselves. I didn't want to face up to the consequences of my actions. I had a wild hair up my ass.

I met my first wife when I was going to junior college, right after the war. She was a high school student, and I was going to junior college at Wilburton. I saw her around. I had bought me a car. I saw her waiting for the bus to school. I asked her if she wanted a ride. She accepted. She knew vaguely of me. I knew her uncle. I'd get drunk with him. I also knew her dad and mom. Anyway, we started riding to school together in my car. Eventually, we got married. Her family didn't like it at all. "His great uncle is a witch. He's probably got witch power too." My sisters were against it for different reasons; they just didn't want to see me marry a White girl. Her mama was very racist and didn't want her to marry an Indian. We were married for 12 years. We had kids together.

The way I see it now and look back on it, neither one of us was worth a damn. We were screwed up. I was upset when she left me, but now I think it was for the best. I don't hold any animosity towards her now. I hated that woman with a passion for taking the kids away from me for a long time. I used to think up ways I would eventually kill her. She just up and ran away with my children, without a word. I have let all that go now. I didn't know where they were until I sobered up. When I sobered up, I went to look for them. I found out where they were after one of them responded to an ad I placed in a paper. They invited me for Christmas. I came by Greyhound to see them.

After my marriage broke up and I lost my kids, I just got, more or less, crazy and crazier—angry! I had learned how to kill, fight, and screw up, get drunk, raise hell. When I got out of the military, I continued to do the same things. It didn't set too well with the general population, the civilians. I can't say all of it was the fault of White people. I can look at it today and say that I got into a lot of trouble due to my misunderstanding and my ignorance. I can't point fingers and say the White people are the cause of me being what I was. I can't point my finger at 'em that way. That would be a cop-out. I just couldn't adjust that well.

My drinking stayed the same for a while, and then it got worse. Alcohol has a progressive tendency. The more you drink, the more you get hooked into it. It takes a period of years to really get down to the point where I got with alcoholism. My life became a lot of fightin', a lot of robbin', a lot of stealin'. I was deep into doin' things for all the wrong reasons. My life was just screwed up altogether, in general. I became a drifter. I would grab me a handful of boxcar and go whenever the notion struck me. There were times I get down to the freight yard, I'd meet a lot of other guys I knew. "Where you going, Beaver?" "Hell, I don't know." "Come on, let's go this way." "Okay, might as well." Once I had a painting job. A guy came by and asked if I wanted to go to Denver. I said, "Sure." I left my brush, paint—everything—and took off. I didn't even go collect my pay or quit. I had no direction. I just didn't care.

You learn how to live on the street the same way as you learn how to stay off the street. You learn these things from people that are doin' it. They learned me a lot on skid row. I learned how to steal. I learned how to rob. I got so good at stealin' and robbin', I used to go to a bar down on Main Street in Stockton. I'd tell this bartender, the guy who owned the bar, "I'mma go down here and steal something, but I need to borrow some money on the strength that I'm gonna steal." He'd loan me the money on my ability to steal. Whenever I got busted and went to jail, I'd go back and explain. He'd say, "You got busted, didn't you?" I'd say, "Yeah." "It's okay. You catch me when you come 'round again." That's the way we functioned. I learned how to function on the street.

I was in my early 40s when I bottomed out. I was a skid row bum. Drinkin' wine every day. If you ever become an alcoholic, you won't go to bed unless you got a bottle to wake up with the next morning. You don't want to go through the shakes and withdrawals. You'll have that bottle with you, to wake up with. I was totally hooked. I'm totally an alcoholic.

I think there was lot of things that made up the whole nucleus of wanting to quit, or knowing I had to quit. My health was part of it. I had a heart attack. I got to the point I couldn't walk. I got arthritis, and my knees got swollen up big round. The winos was carryin' me up and down the street, but that didn't keep me from gettin' drunk and fightin'. My eyesight got bad. I was almost blind. My hearing got bad.

We was drinkin' wine. It's got a lotta sugar in it. It's sweet, so you really don't eat. You eat mostly out of necessity, not because you crave food or you get hungry. You eat because if you don't eat you get sick. Maybe when I got to where I couldn't walk, and those guys had to carry me up and down the street, maybe that was one of the turnin' points in my life. Maybe that had a big influence on it, because I couldn't get around like I did before. I was athletic when I was young. Now I was becoming disabled. I couldn't rob people. I couldn't steal anything. There went my livelihood! That got me to thinking, "I gotta do somethin'." It kinda scared me. It was somewhere 'round 'bout '68 when I sobered up and went into treatment. I was in Stockton, California.[1]

Notes

[1] References on American Indian boarding school experience:
Bosworth, D. (2015). American Indian boarding schools: An exploration of global, ethnic, and cultural cleansing. Mt. Pleasant, NY: Ziibiwing.

Brave Heart, M., et al. (2011). Historical trauma among indigenous people of the Americas: Research and clinical considerations. *Journal of Psychoactive Drugs, 43.*

Evans-Campbell, T. (2008). Historical trauma in American Indian/Alaska Native communities: A multilevel framework for exploring the impact on individuals, families, and communities. *Journal of Interpersonal Violence, 23.*

Lajimodiere, D. (2014). American Indian boarding schools in the United States: A brief history and legacy. In E. Poulou and W. Littlechild (Eds.), *Indigenous peoples' access to justice, truth, and reconciliation.* New York, NY: Columbia University Press.

5

Forced Assimilation and the Creation of the Urban Indian Community

According to the 2010 U.S. Census, 75% of the Indian community resides in urban settings. The urban Indian community is receiving greater recognition as an emerging community in the United States.[1] The biggest migration of American Indians to urban centers began in the 1960s with the federal government's Urban Indian Relocation Program. Indians from throughout the country were enticed to move to selected cities where they were to receive jobs. Many American Indians were living in abject poverty on reservations and were enticed to move to cities for a higher standard of living; however, this promised assistance never materialized, and they lived in urban poverty. Indians moved to relocation centers in Chicago, Cincinnati, Cleveland, Dallas, Denver, Los Angeles, Phoenix, San Francisco, San Jose, and St. Louis. According to the 2010 Census, California has a larger American Indian population than any other state. In addition to being aware of Indian cultural values and the legacy of historical trauma discussed above, the culturally sensitive clinician must have a working knowledge of the urban Indian community structure.

The urban Indian community functions as an intertribal "community without walls." While Indians live in the Bay Area in great numbers, there are not American Indian neighborhoods. In the San Francisco Bay Area's Urban Indian community, one meets individuals (and their children and grandchildren) who relocated from reservation communities during the federal Urban Relocation program; modern-day immigrants from tribal communities in other states, Canada, and Mexico; and, of course, members of tribes indigenous to California.

FIGURE 5.1   2017 Stanford Powwow held in San Francisco Bay Area.

Source: https://www.facebook.com/stanfordpowwow/photos. Copyright © 2017 by Jack Malotte.

Indian people meet at various community events held at local colleges and community organizations. Information about issues affecting the Indian community is often shared informally at such times. This is especially true of the powwow. The word "powwow" is an Algonquin word that means "to meditate." The powwow is an event at which one sees Indians dressed in traditional clothing dancing to drums. Beaver always stressed that one should pray when dancing at the powwow. Powwows profile intertribal social dances. As seen on the 46th annual San Francisco Bay Area Pow Wow flyer below, community is at the heart of the pow wow. The 2017 Stanford Pow Wow was an opportunity for the local Native community to renew social ties and share information about an issue of concern for Native peoples nationally. Stewardship of Nature and the interrelatedness of all creation is a key American Indian cultural value. Prominently placed on this flyer, the words "Water is Life" announced the theme of this gathering. Special honors were awarded to "Water Protectors"—individuals who protested the Dakota Access Pipeline at Standing Rock at risk of personal injury from law enforcement and oil company employees. This is an Indigenous environmental/spiritual movement to keep our waters free of pollution.

In the San Francisco Bay Area's American Indian community, there are people of multiple tribal ancestries (more than one tribe in their ancestry) as well as individuals with mixed racial ancestry (e.g., Caucasian, African, and Asian/Pacific Islander). Mexican American Indian influences are seen at our powwows, which usually have special performances by Aztec dancers. In addition, Grupo Mayo, whose members are Indians from tribes such as the Mayan and Huichol people of Mexico, are active.

Single Chinese men who came to California to work on the construction of the railroads in the 19th century were forbidden by state law to marry White women. Many of them married Indian women instead. Their descendants are still in California.

The Black Native American Association (BNAA), a group of individuals with mixed African American and American Indian ancestry, is also active within this intertribal community. BNAA recently sponsored a large powwow that drew Black Indians from around the country. Others, of all racial mixtures, from the local Indian community also participated. The right of mixed-race individuals to identify primarily with one of their ancestral cultural groups, if they so choose, is supported in culturally sensitive clinical work.[2]

The Bay Area is one of the most socially liberal, inclusive areas of the United States. LGBT (lesbian, gay, bisexual, and transgender) people are valued members of the urban Indian community. They are called "two-spirit" people. The term "two-spirit" is based on a belief held by some tribes that an LGBT person has special spiritual powers due to possessing both a male and a female spirit. Prior to the coming of the Christian missionaries, most Indian peoples were quite tolerant of two-spirit people. A movement to return to this past openness is growing in the Indian community.[3] The organization Bay Area

American Indian Two-Spirits (BAAITS) has been active in the community for 20 years. It has weekly meetings, national retreats for two-spirit people, and a very well-attended national powwow that is popular in all sectors of the American Indian community.

There is a unique role for American Indian therapists who wish to help the community in culturally congruent ways within the urban context. Researchers have documented that traditional Indian healing methods are quite efficacious for a wide range of psychiatric and substance abuse disorders and can be successfully blended with Western counseling techniques.[4]

Substance abuse is a problem within the urban Indian community. In its *2010 National Survey on Drug Abuse and Mental Health*, the federal government's Substance Abuse and Mental Health Services Administration (SAMHSA) indicated that the rate for "substance abuse and any co-occurring mental health disorder" is approximately 8% for American Indians and Alaska Natives; approximately 4% for Caucasians, African Americans, and Hispanics; and about 2% for Asian Americans. This said, it is difficult to offer a precise statistic as to how much alcohol abuse exists among Indians. Published estimates of American Indian alcohol abuse range from 10%–80%. Part of this disparity among statistical reports is due to the fact that the prevalence of alcohol abuse varies by tribe, region, whether individuals are living in rural reservation settings or in urban environments (reservations generally have more alcohol abuse, but there are exceptions), age (teenagers and young adults are more likely to abuse alcohol, and many older adults are totally abstinent), acculturative style (individuals actively involved in traditional ceremonial practices have lower abuse rates), and gender (males generally have higher abuse rates). Clearly, addiction and recovery is a complex phenomenon among Indians.[5]

Substance abuse can be greatly lowered by a concerted effort in local Indian communities to stem the use of alcohol and drugs. In one of the most famous interventions ever documented, the Alkali Lake Reserve of Shuswap Indians in British Columbia reduced the rate of alcohol abuse from virtually 100% to 5% over a 10-year period. Tribal leaders implemented a program to revive traditional forms of spirituality and healing, increased substance abuse treatment services, and implemented a tribal ban on alcohol in public settings. Most urban Indian organizations and powwows ban the use of drugs and alcohol for the common good. This communal ban helps individuals in recovery maintain their sobriety. Alcohol has been and continues to be a challenge in the Indian community, but culturally based intervention projects are making a difference.

Don Coyhis (2002), writing on "walking the red road" and maintaining sobriety, makes an elegant statement in support of tradition-based community-intervention programs to reduce alcohol abuse among American Indians: "Native frameworks of recovery have always been and continue to be framed in terms of an inextricable link between help for the individual and hope for a community. ... Culturally informed treatment seeks to understand the wounded individual in the context of the historical and continued wounding of the Native tribal culture of which he or she is a part."[6] It is noteworthy that while American Indians have the highest addiction rate of any ethnic group, they also have the highest rates of recovery and sobriety of any ethnic group. There is a great deal of community support for sobriety. Most Urban Indian community events have a "no alcohol allowed" policy.

The federal government's past effort at forced assimilation was based in part on encouraging "rugged individualism" The government policy was to get Indians to say mine instead of ours, me instead of us, and I instead of we. Indian identity was and still remains "related identity." Indian identity asks not so much "Who am I?" as "Where do I fit in the greater scheme of life?" Each person has a place just as all plants and animals have a place in the circle of life. Elders encourage community members to discover and be true to themselves but also to relate in a good way to others. There is a Lakota expression often stated by Lakotas (and others) in Indian ceremonies: mitakuye oyasin ("All are my relatives."). Being a good relative is highly valued by Indian people. This includes being a good relative in relationship to other people and to the whole of creation. Indian identity is anchored in relationships. When meeting for the first time, Indians will ask each other for tribal affiliations before asking about profession. For more discussion of the topic of "related identity" in the Indian context, see Jorgenson (1972).[7]

A central theme in Beaver's life was the forced assimilation he underwent in both Oklahoma and California. This chapter will also provide a general background for the assimilation pressures that impacted Beaver's life and the lives of other Indians at the beginning of the 20th century.

The U.S. government's Indian policy at the beginning of the 20th century remained forced assimilation. Tribal government was weak and had limited authority. Nineteenth- and 20th-twentieth century government policy focused on extinguishing Indian culture. The practice of Indian religious ceremonies were outlawed by statute. Special Indian courts were set up to prosecute Indians who were found participating in tribal ceremonies. On some reservations,

Indian medicine bags and other religious objects were confiscated by police or missionaries.

The forced assimilation of Indian people gained renewed vigor in the 1950s and 1960s. Federal policy moved aggressively against the Indian way of life by terminating federal recognition of numerous reservations. The federal Termination Program lead to many tribes losing their territorial land holdings and remuneration promised in past treaties. The stated goal was to turn Indians into red-skinned individualistic Euro-Americans through forced assimilation into mainstream American life.

Upon moving to the cities, most Indians found high unemployment, substandard housing or homelessness, discrimination, and exploitation. Many disillusioned Indian people returned to their tribal communities, but most stayed on and established new lifestyles. Whether they stayed or returned to the reservation, they discovered that the "American Dream" was just that—only a dream. Most Indians who stayed on in cities felt misunderstood by their non-Indian neighbors. Some suffered the "Last of the Mohicans Syndrome," a sense that they were the only Indians left. Indians in urban settings in the 1960s lived at the bottom of the social ladder. They felt that non-Indians looked down on them. This was the same generation of Indians who survived

FIGURE 5.2   Teenage boys hanging out: Intertribal Friendship House, Oakland 1972.

the boarding school experience. Now, as adults, they faced new trauma in adjusting to a foreign lifestyle in cities. Some coped with this turmoil by abusing alcohol and drugs. Some of the earliest meeting places for Indians living in cities were Indian bars.

Instead of successfully integrating Indian people into American society, these policies guaranteed a generation that lacked social and psychological stability. These policies did not exist in a vacuum. Indians had survived genocidal wars, slavery, epidemics brought on by contact with White society, broken treaties, and loss of tribal lands. It is small wonder that there are higher rates of depression, suicide, and alcoholism in 20th-century Indian communities than in the rest of the United States. It is a tribute to Beaver that he overcame these social obstacles after a period of confusion and addiction and dedicated his life to improving the overall quality of life in the Indian community.

With the emergence of the Red Power movement in the 1960s, relocated Indians started networking and building community structures. They created organizations (such as the Intertribal Friendship House in Oakland, California) that could help them thrive in the urban environment. The migration to the cities encouraged the creation of a new pan-Indian identity. This was the first time Indians from scores of different tribes lived in the same vicinity. An intertribal Indian community formed. Even Indians whose tribes were traditional enemies worked together for a common cause.

In the cities, a new identity, "the Indian," was born. Indian people had previously seen themselves primarily as members of particular tribes, but increasingly, people also saw themselves as part of a newly emerging pan-Indian ethnic minority group. The concept of being "Indian" took on more value as increasing numbers of Indians began to marry and have children with members of other tribes, creating a new intertribal identity. This trend has continued to the present day.

As previously noted, the urban Indian community in the San Francisco Bay Area is a community of informal contacts—a community without walls. The community comes together for holiday celebrations, memorial services, pow-wows, arts and crafts classes, talking circles, community dinners, and to hear Indian speakers visiting local college campuses or community organizations. There is a cross-fertilization between urban and reservation communities. Many urban Indians return to tribal communities throughout the United States, Canada, and Mexico to attend ceremonies. Medicine people and Peyote road leaders come to urban centers to conduct ceremonies. There are intertribal sweat lodge ceremonies that bring community members together. There are also Indian Christian churches.

In the 1960s and 1970s, Indian activists forced changes in government policy toward Indians. The government began funding social service organizations focused on the problems of Indians in urban settings. Organizations were established to promote the welfare of Indian children, create educational and vocational opportunities, promote and maintain sobriety, and provide health care. Beaver and other Indian community leaders started organizations such as the Native American Health Center, Three Rivers Indian Lodge, Friendship House Association of San Francisco, Intertribal Friendship House of Oakland, and San Francisco Indian Center. Indians employed in these organizations and elsewhere formed formal and informal service networks.

One of the greatest challenges for Indians who migrated to cities was maintaining an Indian way of life. The intertribal cultural institutions and activities that developed helped to reinforce Indian lifeways. The development of a pan-Indian identity led to an open, incorporative, and welcoming attitude toward diversity. This may have been the natural by-product of having a multitribal community. In addition, many in the second and third generations are products of interracial marriages. This is no doubt a reflection of the San Francisco Bay Area's status as one of the most politically liberal areas of the United States, well known for its openness to diversity.

This welcoming attitude in the urban Indian community is seen in the greater willingness to accept self-identification as Indian as sufficient proof of Indian ancestry (to be sure, this tolerant attitude is not universally held by all in the community). The general attitude in the community seems to be that if a person states they have Indian ancestry, participates in community functions, and shows an understanding and acceptance of pan-Indian cultural values, then he or she is accepted as Indian—whether formally enrolled or not. The urban community is also more welcoming of those who have been cut off from their tribal traditions—such as those adopted out to White families by force. There is also a greater acceptance of Indians whose ancestors fully assimilated to the White culture, some to the point of not even telling their children they have Indian ancestry. These individuals are often trying to find their way back to an "Indian" identity.

Indians in the urban environment struggle to maintain healthy families and community support networks as they recover from the impact of historical traumas. They do this within the context of the larger non-Indian community, which has little knowledge of Indian customs and values. Non-Indians tend to hold stereotypic images of Indians. Some non-Indians idealize Indian ways, while others denigrate Indians. Urban Indians succeed at maintaining positive ethnic identities to the extent that they can maintain viable Indian cultural ties and identities while navigating the stresses of adapting to mainstream American society.

Beaver moved to the intertribal community of the greater San Francisco Bay Area's intertribal community in the 1960s, the time of its earliest formation. He changed and grew as the community developed. He actively contributed to the development of an intertribal Indian community that worked for the well-being of all. He made the transition from seeing himself only in tribal terms as Choctaw. He broadened his identity to embrace membership in the new pan-Indian world. He endeavored to combine what he had learned from his great uncle, a Choctaw medicine man, with the practices of other Indian people he met in the urban environment. He decided to help all Indians regardless of tribal or racial mixture, or enrollment status. He knew that a return to traditional Indian values would heal and renew the urban Indian community.

Before going further, it is appropriate before proceeding to briefly discuss the term ""traditional"" Indian as it is used throughout this text. As Beaver once said to me, no Indians today live entirely as their ancestors did. Few would be willing to part with their refrigerators or automobiles in order to be deemed traditional by others. I use the term "traditional," in much the same way as did Beaver: to refer to Indian people who desire to adhere to pre-contact Indian cultural values and ceremonial practices. He said, "We want the modern inventions of the White people, but we don't want to accept White values like loving money more than other people or the land." Many modern-day Indian people want to lead an authentic Indian lifestyle, true to Indian values. There is real fear that authentic Indian lifestyles will vanish.

Notes

1 Witko, T. (2006). *Mental health care for urban Indians*. Washington, DC: American Psychological Association.

Le Grand, J. (2002). *Indian metropolis*. Urbana, IL: University of Illinois Press.

Fixico, D. (2000). *op. cite*

Lobo, S. (1998). op. cite

2 Root, M. (Ed.). (1996). *The multiracial experience: Racial borders as the new frontier.* Newbury Park, CA: SAGE.

3 Gilley, B. (2010). Native American sexual inequalities: American Indian cultural conservative homophobia and the problem the problem of tradition. *Sexualities, 13.*

Jacobs, S., Thomas, W., & Lang, S. (1997). *Two Spirit people: Native American gender identity, sexuality, and spirituality.* Urbana, IL: University of Illinois Press.

Erdoes, R., & Lame Deer. (1994). *Lame Deer, seeker of visions.* New York, NY: Pocket.

4 Gone, J. (2011). The Red Road to wellness: Cultural reclamation in a First Nations community treatment center. *American Journal of Community Psychology, 47.*

Trimble, J. (2010). The virtues of cultural resonance, competence, and relational collaboration with Native American communities: A synthesis of the counseling and psychotherapy literature. *The Counseling Psychologist, 38.*

5 Chartier, K., & Caetano, R. (2010). Ethnicity and health disparities in alcohol research. *Alcohol Research and Health, 33.*

6 Coyhis, D., & White, W. (2002). Alcohol problems in Native America: Changing paradigms and clinical practice. *Alcohol Treatment Quarterly, 20.*

Guillory, B., Willey, E., & Duran, E. (1998). Analysis of a community organizing case study: Alkali Lake., *Journal of Rural Psychology, 9.*

7 Jorgenson, J. (1972). *The Sun Dance religion: Power for the powerless.* Chicago, IL: University of Chicago Press.

6

Recovery, Reconciliation, and Indian Community Revitalization

As our conversation progressed, Beaver spoke about the events that led to his recovery from drug and alcohol abuse and the factors that have helped him maintain sobriety for over 40 years. Beaver came to see that substance abuse was a widespread problem in the Indian community and that it has a detrimental impact on the quality of life of Indian adults and their children. He saw his own recovery as interlocked with promoting sobriety throughout the Indian community.

Beaver offered his philosophy of substance abuse treatment. He argued that it works best for American Indians when it is based on traditional Indian cultural values. He also believed that recovery is more likely to succeed when all community gatherings are drug and alcohol free.

Beaver had moved from being angry at the world to being a genuinely caring and self-sacrificing person. He detailed his early efforts to start Three Rivers Indian Lodge, an American Indian residential program for the treatment of substance abuse that still exists today in Manteca, California. His altruism is shown in his working without a salary for the first 4 years of the program's operation.

By midlife, Beaver had returned to the spiritual practices of his medicine man uncle. He led ceremonies. He also helped to start a Gourd Clan Society in order to promote sobriety in the community.

Beaver:

This Indian woman had a treatment program, and she asked some of her residents, "Who is that little Indian I see all up on his feet fightin' in China Park—fightin', and robbin' people and stealin' things? Who is he?" They told her, "That's Beaver." She said, "I'd like to talk to him." They said, "Don't even try. He might talk to you, and again he might cuss you out. That's one bad little Indian dude. I don't think he'll ever quit his way." She said, "Well, I want to talk to him anyway."

She asked one of the residents there to go with her, and they found me sittin' on the corner. He came over, and he said, "This lady over here wants to talk to you." I said, "She can talk all she wants to, as long as she buys me a fifth of wine." He went back and told her. He says, "He'll talk to you, but you gotta buy a fifth of wine." She said, "Well, maybe he'll get drunk, and I won't get to talk to him." He says, "That is the law down here. If you're buyin', he'll listen to you. You can ask him anything you want to, and he'll talk to you. When that bottle runs out, if you still want to talk, you better buy another bottle! As long as you're buyin', these people will listen to you."

She told him, "You go in there and get a fifth of wine, and give it to him and tell him I want to talk to him." He went and got the wine, brought it to me, and says, "Come on over here. She wants to talk to you." When you got the bottle, there's two or three people following you, because they want to drink out of that bottle too. We all went over there. She says, "Well, I want to help you." I said, "You already have. You got me a fifth of wine." I asked, "What else you want?" She said, "What would you say if I offer to take you to a treatment program?" I said, "I'd tell you to go to hell. I don't want to go to no damn treatment program." She said, "Well, I run this one. It's not run by the county, and it's not run by the state. It's run by me." I asked, "What's the catch?" She said, "First I got to take you over here to the welfare department and sign you up so I can get paid for what I'm gonna do for you. You don't have to worry about it. There'll be nobody comin' 'round to talk to you except me and one of my counselors." I said, "Well, I'll go talk to 'em, but I'm not gonna promise you I'll go into treatment."

I went in down there to the program, and I was settin' there waitin'. One of these guys come through there that I knew. I had been in prison with him, and I had been on the street with him. He asked, "Beaver what the hell are you doing here?" I said, "These damn fools is tryin' to get me to go into the treatment program." He said, "That might not be a bad idea. What treatment program are you going into?" I had a card in my pocket. I handed it to him and said, "This one. This Indian lady got this treatment program here." He said, "I'm the treatment director there. That's a good program." I asked, "You're treatment director? You quit drinkin'?" He says, "Yeah." I said, "Bullshit! You didn't quit drinkin'!" He said, "Yeah, I did. I've turned my life around. It's a different ball game." I says, "Okay, I'll go. I'll go with you to that one."

It was Flora Street Alcohol Treatment Program in Stockton, California. I went into that treatment program, but I still thought he was connin' me. I knew him when he was on the street, when we was in prison together. He was altogether a different kind of character than what he was tellin' me he was. I didn't think he could ever get his life together. The more I watched him, the more I become convinced that he had changed.

FIGURE 6.1 The San Francisco Bay Area.

Source: Rand McNally & Co., 1911.

I guess he was the main turnin' point in my life to show me that, hey, regardless what you've done, or how you been, you can make that change. That was the beginning of the turnaround. That was the beginning of me really lookin' at my life. I knew that those people had something that I didn't have, and I wanted to find out what it was. Levi Murdock, he was a Indian from Oklahoma—I think he was Soc and Fox—he told me, "Beaver, you got to find spirituality." He says, "You find that one, and I guarantee you'll have that sobriety that you're lookin' for." It took me a while for that one to sink in. I got through the program in about 18 months.

In the meantime, ol' Bob Roberts was goin' through a program. He was another Choctaw from Oklahoma. He was gettin' sobered up. We used to talk about, while we was still drinkin' and getting' drunk, how we wanted to do something to help the Indian people. Then when we sobered up we got together, and that's when we come to the conclusion that an alcohol program for Indian people was needed. We had come to the conclusion alcohol and drugs was a big problem in the Indian community. We started puttin' the San Joaquin Council of American Indians together. Our main objective was to start a treatment program for Indian people. We knew a lot of our old drunken, drinkin' partners was Indian. Most of them were. They hung out down at China Park in Stockton. They were from all different tribes. From all the way up north and from all the way back from Oklahoma, from all over the United States they was comin' in. We wanted to help 'em.

Some of the local Indian community was more into other type things, so we told 'em, "We're gonna put a alcohol and drug treatment program together. That's our main focus." Some of 'em wanted a Indian Center. There was a lot of programs that these other people were lookin' at. We said, "You guys find your committee, and put it together. Start workin' on it. Write your grant, and get what you need. We're workin' on this one, on a alcohol and drug treatment program." Some of 'em worked on projects for a while. The government wasn't too quick to give any of us money, so they kinda fizzled out. They got tired of workin' on their program, because it wasn't comin' together the way they thought it would. Bob, Levi, and myself, we kept workin' at this one. We just kept goin', kept goin', kept goin', and kept goin'.

We got started when I was in that treatment program with that Indian woman. She asked me what I wanted to do, and I explained to her what our goals were. She said—she was a Christian woman—she belonged to some church that was sending her to India to teach people how to be good Christians. She said, "When I go there, if you and Bob are still interested in doin' what you're talkin' about, everything in this house, everything I got here, you and Bob can have. All you got to do is find your house. I'll even move it for you." I went to AA [Alcoholics Anonymous], and I told the AA people what I was lookin' for and what I was gonna do. They found a house for me. They called me and told me, and I went down there and rented the house. That Indian lady was true to her word. She hired a truck, and they went in and packed everything up. Everything that was in there we got. Even to the toilet paper. We opened that house up.

I was gettin' total disability. I was usin' my check from disability to pay for rent, utilities, and lights. The whole thing. I think it's something like $125 for a house (that was way back). My utilities wasn't that much. I was only gettin' something like a hundred and something dollars, but it covered all our costs. The county was giving me, through the state rehab, $125 for every client I had. That $125 paid for the food that we needed. I had enough from my SSI and my disability to pay for the rent and the utilities. I wasn't makin' no salary at all for the first 4 years.

Whenever I got all these checks or got cash, I would open up a desk drawer and put all that money in an envelope. A lot of money. I had food money, electric money, telephone money, all our utilities, everything. I told everybody in the house, "This is not my house. This is not my money. This is your house. This is your money. If we don't use it right, we all are out. When the first of the month comes around," I says, "You know how to pay these bills. Make sure these bills get paid. The money's all in there, in each one of these envelopes." It was kind of a community-type thing. Everybody done exactly what they should have done. When a bill come due, they got the bill with the due date on it. They taken care of it, because the money was there. We had no problems. When the rent come due, our landlord lived just up the street from us. They took it up there and said, "Here's the rent money." *My philosophy is that if you treat people like they are trustworthy, they will not betray your trust.*

One year I went to Oklahoma. When I got back, those guys, I don't know how they done it, they said, "Beaver, we saved a hundred dollars while you was gone. We thought you might need it. We saved it." I said, "I don't know how in the hell you guys done that." They said, "Well, we did." The cook told me what they done. They cut all these coupons and things. They used a lot of those coupons every time they went to the store. I saw what we were doing as a community thing.

There was this kid. His mama and his daddy both was alcoholics. I knew them. She was Sioux, and he was Choctaw. They got arrested for being drunken there in the park. The cops there in China Park, they seen the little guy runnin' 'round, and they brought him over to my house. They said, "Beaver, we know you used to drink with his mama and his stepdad. They both got put in jail, and drunk. This little boy don't have nowhere to go." I said, "Just leave him here. We'll take care of 'im."

It was good for the men that was there, because they all taken up donations amongst themselves. They bought him a bicycle. One of 'em volunteered to take him to a show every Saturday. They spent the weekend with him. They'd buy him clothes. They really treated that little guy. They learned how to share and care for another human bein'. The social workers used to come stay a while and just sit around and talk. They said, "It's real good that you got a place like this, because these men are learning something. They're learning how to share and care for another human bein'." When they finally got around to sendin' that person from Washington down to check our treatment program out, they asked us about our policy. They seen what we were doin' and how we were doin' it. They liked it. They bought it. They told us, "You send your grant application in." We sent our application in for $147,000, and that's what we got. We didn't get the grant until '75.

Jeannette Hendricks (Cherokee), former client, employee, and close friend

In 1974, I went to Bret Heart hospital to the alcoholic ward and was up there for 3 weeks. One of my counselors called me into his office, introduced me to this little guy, and told me he was going to be our speaker that day. After talking to this guy for a while, Sonny asked him if I was going to stay sober, and Beaver said, "*No.*" I looked at him and didn't like him. [Author's note: Beaver recalls this meeting.

He said he told her she would not stay sober to get her mad enough to prove him wrong.]

The next year my mother died of cancer, and I was so lost I knew I would have to move out of Tracy, California, because I couldn't stay sober there. A friend of mine, Sally, came over to Tracy and picked me up. She took me to Stockton, California, and we went to Beaver's halfway house. I talked to Beaver, and he told me to move in there. I asked him how this was going to affect his other clients, and he said he didn't care because I was pregnant and had two little girls. A week later I showed up on his doorstep, and he opened the door and said, "Come on in." My youngest daughter just looked up at him and said, "Are you going to be my grandpa?" His answer was, "Do you want me to be?" We moved in, and he has been her grandpa ever since.

I didn't know much about Indians although I am one-quarter Cherokee. I learned a lot from Beaver, and I also learned if I wanted to stay sober I had to do some things I didn't want to do. I was eventually hired as a cook. This house was like no other house I have ever seen. It was open 24 hours a day, and the coffee pot went 24 hours a day. If anyone came in and was hungry, Beaver would wake me up and have me fix them something to eat. He would say, "Come on. Someone needs us."

At first I thought he had some ideas. One night when he came home, I told him we had to talk. He sat down, and I fixed his plate and got him some coffee and asked, "Is it true that you want to go to bed with me?" He said, "Well, what would you think of that if that was true?" I told him that I had never trusted any man in my life, but I did him. I felt that if I slept with him I would lose that trust. He said, "Okay, then we will leave things like they are."

He made me drive to San Francisco once because I told him I couldn't drive on the freeway. It was a good con job on his part. He told me to drive and let him sleep for a while, knowing once I got down the road I wouldn't be able to pull over.

I had been to powwows when I was a kid in South Dakota, but I never knew the real meaning of them. I thought we were just having fun. Through Beaver, I learned that it was so much more than just having fun. It was a spiritual thing, and I could pray to my Creator. Powwows mean so much to me now. I have become a powwow dancer.

Beaver stole all my kids' hearts, and they still think of him as their grandpa after 28 years. My son is 27 years old now. He was born thinking Beaver was his grandpa, and nothing has changed. Beaver has seen me sober and he has seen me drunk, but the love between us just keeps growing. When he told me he was moving back to Oklahoma last year, I got panicky and I had to go over and stay with him for a week to tell him just how much he meant to me. He is the dad I never knew.

My grandfather was a medicine man, but I did not know him well. Beaver is the one man in my life that I have trusted, and he has never told me a lie. He has always been straightforward with me, and he is that way with everyone. God has been so good to me by putting Beaver in my life, and when I met him, all I had to my name were two girls, a big stomach, and two black garbage bags of clothes. He took me in.

We started our treatment program in '79. It was Stockton Indian Lodge at the beginning. When we moved up where it is now in Manteca, we called it Three Rivers Indian Lodge. Our basic principle is the AA philosophy: try to maintain sobriety, and try to help another human being achieve sobriety. We knew we couldn't do that without a spiritual entity. That's when we got off into the spiritual things.

We had all these Indians comin' from all walks of life, from all over the United States, and some of 'em knew about the medicine. Some of them knew about medicine men. We had medicine people come in before we had the Gourd Society. They'd come in and do the ceremonies, pipe ceremonies, or whatever. As we grew, we put in a sweat lodge. We put a hogan in, and eventually the Black Wolf Gourd Clan Society. We also started the powwow at Three Rivers.

When I was in charge of the Three Rivers Indian Lodge, I would take any race, but I kept more Indians. It is essential we keep our spiritual societies what they are, "Indian societies," but not really say that another race of persons cannot be a member of that society and have the same rights and privileges that the Indians have; however, the majority should be Indian.

Initially, we went back to the Kiowas for help. They brought the Gourd Clan Society out in the open right after World War II. They had Kiowas coming out of the service, and they were getting in lots of trouble. They were going crazy and being thrown in the nuthouse for alcoholism. They were suffering from what they had seen in the war and what they had done in the war. They were having quite a bit of trouble. The Kiowas brought the Gourd Clan out in order to give them a spiritual foundation so they might be able to deal with their problems in a more solid way. They gave them war veterans something to grasp onto.

We also started our society to help Indians deal with personal problems and alcoholism. We started our society to help people at Three Rivers Indian Lodge alcohol treatment program. I had a friend who was also a drug abuse counselor. We would go to AA meetings a lot, and we would sit in his office or my office and talk about how we could help these recovering alcoholics. They weren't getting much out of AA, and they didn't want to go to a Christian church. We decided that we needed to find a traditional Indian way to help these Indians. This was about '78. He asked, "Can you get permission from San Joaquin Council of American Indians to put in a Gourd Society?" I didn't know anything about a Gourd Society, so I asked him, "What is it?" He said, "That is a spiritual society that is going to help these people overcome alcoholism." I knew I needed something more than AA, but I wasn't ready to make that lifetime commitment. Even though I was sober, I wasn't ready to give up everything. I asked him if I could have 2 weeks to think this over. He said, "I want you to think it over. It's a lifetime commitment."

Two weeks later, I went to him and told him I was ready to make that commitment. He asked me to ask permission from the San Joaquin Council of American Indians to put a Gourd Clan Society in. They wanted to know what a Gourd Clan Society is. I told them it was a spiritual entity like a church, but wasn't a church. They asked me if I could avoid making a political thing out of it. We told them we are not in it for political gain. We are in it to help recovering alcoholics get a foundation, a solid foundation in spiritual life. We wanted to show them how to have fun and enjoy life without getting drunk, without using alcohol and drugs. Abstinence is about not drinking and drugging. *Sobriety is about finding that inner joy so you no longer want to use and abuse substances.*

The San Joaquin Council of American Indians agreed to let us use their nonprofit number to get started. The Director of Three Rivers Indian Lodge told us, "Make sure it's an option to be part of this if they want to. Don't force anyone." Most of them who chose to go the Gourd Clan way stayed sober. We got permission from Star Hawk. That is a Gourd Society. They informed us that we could use their format but couldn't name our society Star Hawk. We had to find our own name and put our own society together.

To start a Gourd Clan Society, you have to get permission from the elders of an existing society. You couldn't just up and start one. My friend already knew their protocol. He was Cheyenne-Arapaho. He gave us a lot of information. We got a lot of information from others, people from Oklahoma that was members of the society. We were intertribal. We couldn't set up a tribal society because of what we had at Three Rivers Indian Lodge. We were getting people of different tribes coming in. We couldn't say this is Choctaw Society or this is a Cheyenne Society. Three Rivers Indian Lodge was intertribal.

When I was a kid growing up, I thought Choctaw was the only Indians there were. When I went to Jones's Academy, I met other tribal people. Drinking alcohol and doing drugs, I drank with everybody and anybody who had a jug. Where we set the Three Rivers Indian Lodge up, we went the intertribal way. On skid row, they share bottles. If you have a bottle, it don't make no difference who you are, Indian or non-Indian, you passed that jug around. Around Stockton, it was kind of intertribal, but you get out of Stockton, you get over up around Tuolumne, you get the Miwoks. We were getting a lot of migratory workers. Indians from other areas— they worked the crops in the Central Valley. If you call it a Choctaw organization, you're going to offend some of the people. Normally you could help, but they wouldn't come because of that name. They would say, "That's a bunch of Choctaw." We got people of all different tribes in our society.

Indian people—now this has been my experience—when I go to a new place I never been before, the first thing I ask is, "Where do the Indians hang out?" They tell me where it's at, and I go find the Indian people. You get to want to be with your own type of people. It don't make no difference if he was Chicano, Sioux, Cheyenne, or Arapaho, as long as he claim to be Indian, I'm happy to see him. Now you take back in Oklahoma in the Choctaw Nation, the intertribal way would not work too good. Here in California and in big cities, it works real good. I would say it is a necessity for Indian people here. This is how the powwow started out here in California.

In the past, you had to be an enrolled Indian to be a member of a Gourd Clan Society. In our society, Wolf Spirit Society, you don't have to be enrolled. Some societies even required you to speak your language and to be a veteran. In our society, you don't need to be a veteran or speak your tribal language. All you got to do is be willing to help another human being to find that spiritual path. You can allow non-Indians to be members; however, my experience with the White folks is they really don't want to learn Indian culture, and they really don't want to change that much. When you got a majority of White people in your society, they seem to want to take over and do things in their cultural ways.

Before we started alcohol-free powwows at Three Rivers Indian Lodge, there'd only be drunken powwows. Even at Stanford University, we was havin' drunken powwows. I went to one in San Jose where they had a big drunken powwow. They had the police department and the whole nine yards—sheriff and everything—out there, breakin' up drunken brawls and drunken fights. They even got in fights with the police. Whenever we started that powwow in Three Rivers, it came out that we was gonna have a powwow, people said, "You can't do that." I didn't know why we couldn't do it. "Well, it's what the powwow is. There will be alcohol, and they will get drunk and they'll fight." We said, "We're not going to allow no alcohol, no drugs, no fights." They still thought it couldn't be done.

We had a hard time convincing the board that we could pull this one off. I talked to Dennis Banks of AIM [American Indian Movement], and he said, "Yeah, we'll pull security for 'ya. How tight do you want it?" I said, "Tight. If you see me walking across there, I got a beer in my hand, run me off, throw me out, or call the law. You see the director of this program come in there drinkin', call the law, throw 'im out. It don't make no difference who they are. You call the law. If you see a bum, he's here drinkin'. He's got alcohol. You call the law. That goes for our head dancers and everybody. Don't leave no one out. This drinking has got to go." We had to make the powwow safe for our children and families. We did have to throw a few people out. I enforced these rules even on my own brother. He was the cook, and he came in drunk, so I fired him. We had to set principles down. We had to hang with 'em, regardless of where it fell. *You have to hang with those principles!*

What we did at powwows influenced not only Northern California but powwows in Southern California too. Soon, they stopped drinking at powwows.

It started here. Now, if you notice on the sign, "No Alcohol, No Drugs." It used to not be stated. It wasn't advertised that way. It had quite a impact on the community as a whole. Anywhere you go you can feel that impact. What is good about it is that you know your kids are gonna be safe. You don't have to tolerate those drunks.

To heal the community, this is important: *You gotta get everybody involved in trying to promote sobriety.* If you can get enough adults committed into sobriety, no drinkin', no druggin', it's gonna have an impact on the community as a whole. They gonna have a impact on their kids, and their kids is gonna have a impact on other kids they meet, and those kids is gonna go back and have an impact on their parents.

I know by my own experience, and by the experience that people I was runnin' with that had alcohol problems, that whenever we'd go get drunk or go out drinking, I noticed everybody made a point to get the kids something. We'd buy 'em soda pop, candy, bologna, and lunchmeats—instead of taking that money and buyin' steak and potatoes or something that was more nourishing.

We were savin' money by buyin' this and not steak and potatoes. We was usin' that money to buy alcohol. *The kids were gettin' deprived.* I see that as deprivation of the kids.

I used to have a sweat lodge right down here in the back of the barn in Turlock. It was a druggy place. I wondered, I always did wonder, "Why'd the Creator send me here? Why am I here runnin' sweats? The mama and the papa and all their friends is comin' round doing drugs." Later on I got my answer. I wasn't there for the mama and the papa. I was there for the kids.

The first day I was there, a mama was all high on drugs, and she asked if I would mind her bringing the kids over. I said, "Nah. Load 'em up. Bring 'em in the pickup." She brought 'em all over here. Those kids, they thought we was rich. We'd taken them in there, and we told them, "Anytime you kids get hungry, you come to this icebox. Anything you see in there that you want to eat, you eat it. Anything that's in that refrigerator, you eat. You don't have to ask permission to go in there and eat it. It's there for that reason and for that purpose." The kids asked, "Are ya'll rich?" I said, "No, we're not." They said, "How do you keep all this food in here?" It made me aware of the way I used to do things and the way I'm doin' 'em now. I see now how we deprived kids by just bringin' 'em junk food.

In the Indian community, alcoholism often goes back several generations. A woman read in the paper that Three Rivers Indian Lodge was doing outreach. She brought her daughter to our outreach program, and I was assigned to be her counselor. Through talkin' to the daughter, I realized her mother also had a alcohol problem. I knew that I had to try to help the mother in order to help the daughter. When I got started talking to the mama, I realized, "Hey, I gotta go farther back than this. I gotta go back to Grandma." That's where the alcohol problem started, with Grandma. In order to help the teenager, she had to be 16 at that particular time, I also had to help the grandma to overcome her addiction to alcohol.

I see that as you gotta go all the way back to find the root of the problem and work it out. You might have to go back, all the way back to the grandma, and chances are the great grandma had the same problem. They are probably dead and gone by now. You start with the farthest one, farthest back that you can get. That's what we done.

I see alcohol addiction as the biggest downfall to the Indian people, more than lack of education, job skills, or anything like that. I see alcoholism as the root of why the Indian people are the lowest man on the totem pole. Out of all the minorities in the United States, we are the minority of the minorities, but when it comes to drinkin' and druggin', we're the majority of the minorities. We have a bigger alcohol and drug problem as a people than any other group of people there is. I think that we have such a big problem because, first of all, we don't understand the related problems that alcohol brings to us. To me, alcohol and drug addiction is our primary problem.

What has helped me is going back to the traditional values and the spiritual principles. These are the meat with the potatoes. This is where the meat is at. It is how you define what you really want to gear into. Indian traditions is what is going to help that Indian person overcome alcohol and drug addiction and help him become a better human bein'. Not only to himself but to his maker, to God as he understands Him, and to another human bein', and to the community as a whole. He'll be a better parent, be a better daddy or a mama, whatever the case might be. Be a better grandparent, grandpa or grandma, whatever the case might be. He'll just become a better human bein'. I tried AA. To be honest with you, I was lookin' for spiritual values, and I found AA was lackin'. They got good values, good principles, but when it come to spiritual things, to me, they wasn't quite reachin' it.

When I was asked to help with putting the Gourd Clan Society in, I knew I needed that extra push, that extra pump, so to speak, to achieve that spiritual part of me that needed fulfillin'. It scared me at first. I said,

"I gotta think about this for a while." There was some things I wanted to do. I knew if I become a spiritual human bein' I couldn't do them things anymore. I knew if I wanted to stay sober I had to have that extra spiritual push. I'm talking about Indian values. Indian spirituality.

To the people who wanted to come into Three Rivers Indian Lodge, I told them it's very simple. I just tell 'em straight out, "We got a sweat lodge. We got a hogan. We got a gourd dance. We got a powwow. We're Indian orientated. We cook Indian. We sleep Indian. We eat Indian. Everything about us is Indian. We are Indians, only we're different tribes. Whenever you come into our program, you gotta be willing to accept our Indian ways, our Indian strengths, and our Indian B.S.—we just Indians. If you can accept it, great! Maybe we can help you. If you can't accept it, don't even try it, 'cuz it won't work for you. Look for another program."

At first we was under United AAA. I don't know what AAA stands for. They weren't too particular about who we served as long as we were serving people. Then the federal government pushed us over onto Indian Health. We got a letter from the President of the United States, which happened to be Ronald Reagan at that time, stating the fact that this was Indian-allocated money and it could only be used to treat Indian people; therefore, they had to have a roll number and meet all the federal guidelines to qualify as a Indian. I thought that was terrible! An alcoholic is an alcoholic. I don't care what color he is or what race he is. If he has a problem with alcohol or drugs, he has a problem. It should be left up to that person to choose where to go. I don't think the government has a right to step in and say, "You can only work with these people or those people, if you have a problem." Also, not all Indians are enrolled.

The first thing I started doing for people and with people was puttin' that Three Rivers Indian Lodge together and working on their alcohol and drug problem. Substance abuse is one hard thing to overcome. I know, because I'm a recovering alcoholic myself. You try to talk to the people. You try to live a life so they could see there is a reality in what you're saying. We have some kind of impact, some kind of influence on people we don't even know. Maybe some little guy, maybe some kids, or grown people; we don't know who. We should present an image to these people that's clean, sober, and livin' the spiritual way.

When I first started counselin', I realized that they were asking me questions I didn't have the answers to. I knew I needed some more schoolin', so I went to University of the Pacific. I went there to get my certification to learn more about alcohol and drugs because I wanted to help these people. I felt bad when they'd ask me some things that I didn't really know the answers to. After I finished UOP, I come to find out that basically your own experience with drugs and alcohol is mainly—and how you overcame addiction—is mainly what an addicted person wants to hear anyway. They don't want to hear this lingo about the name of the disease or the terminology of what it does to the body.

I told them recovering alcoholics, "Whatever it takes for you to stay sober, then by all means do that one. Now you might have to climb up a tree and hang there like a monkey for an hour. Do that, but don't ask me to climb up that tree and hang like a monkey with you; but if that's what you've got to do to stay sober, you do it. You do whatever it takes in order to stay sober."

When you go into treatment to overcome alcohol and drugs, if you're a male, you don't pick a female for a sponsor, and vice versa for females. You don't pick somebody who you could get sexually involved with. You don't pick somebody that hasn't got too much sobriety. You pick somebody that's been sober and working the program for about 10 or 12 years. Get that person to sponsor you.

When you get a hold of your sponsor, he's going to tell you some things that you've got to do in order to stay sober, in order to overcome your addiction and for you to get stronger. One is to turn your will and your life over to God the way you understand Him. Most recovering alcoholics and most alcoholics don't like to hear that, basically because they've had bad experiences with churches. We're not *religiously* inclined. We are *spiritually* inclined. We overcome obstacles through spirituality. We get strong through spirituality. I have yet to find a person who has successfully stayed sober unless they find God the way they understand Him. Those that has found Him, they've got 10, 15, 20, 25, 30 years sobriety. Those I knew that hasn't found Him, most those people died at a young age. I'm not saying this to scare anyone into spirituality. I'm saying this in order that you find something that'll save your life.

We are a part of a greater spiritual plan. I'm not my brother's keeper, I'm my brother's helper. I help him with his plan. Help your brothers and sisters to overcome alcohol and drug addiction. Help them in any way you can.

Betty Cooper (Blackfeet) is the former director
of a substance abuse program for Indian women
in Oakland, California. She now resides in Browning,
Montana on the Blackfeet Reservation

I met Beaver in the late 1970s. I attended the Three Rivers Lodge
campout powwow in July. I went to the sweat lodge ceremony, and
Beaver was the sweat lodge leader. I was so impressed with the strong
message, "Your sobriety is the most important thing. Without sobriety,
you cannot do anything." I learned that Beaver set up the first treatment
lodge for alcohol and other drugs for Native men of all tribes. This
was in Stockton. Then later the lodge was moved to Manteca as Three
Rivers Lodge. I spent valuable time with Beaver over the next 17 years.
I learned all I could from him on how to operate an alcohol and drug
treatment center based in Indian spirituality.

There are activities that I would like to share about Beaver. One was
the building of the medicine arbor at White Cloud Lodge in Oakland.
I was the director there for 10 years. We had the sweat lodge built and
used it two or three times a week. It was for the clients who were in
the 90-day treatment program. We needed an additional ceremonial
arbor for other kinds of spiritual ceremonies. The program served all
tribes, and we tried hard to bring in medicine men and women who
were from the tribe of the current clients in the treatment program. We
needed the arbor for this purpose and for other resource people who
could bring benefits to the clients' Red Road to Recovery. We initially
asked computer experts to use their programs to design the arbor. They
tried to come up with a computer-generated design that would work
for us, but in spite of their good intentions, modern technology failed
to do this correctly. I telephoned Beaver next and explained what we
needed. I invited him to come and stay with us to work out a plan for
this ceremonial arbor.

I remember how Beaver found the middle point of the arbor and
drove a wooden stake into the spot. He took a long length of cord

material and made the outer perimeter of the arbor. The clients marked all this with stakes and twine.

Everybody was involved. We had a happy time building the arbor. Beaver supervised us each step of the way. The first ceremony in the arbor was with Beaver. This was a very spiritual, happy time. In the program, we had clients who were carpenters and roofers—they did all the work.

The second activity that I will share is the making of a video, *The Red Road to Recovery*. The Alameda County alcohol and drug program office received special funds to have treatment programs in Alameda County, California to make their own instructional video using the clients as scriptwriters, role-playing, and camera operators. The White Cloud Lodge (for men) and New Dawn Lodge (for women) chose to do their video on the use of the sweat lodge in the treatment program. The clients all wanted Beaver to be in the video. They had great affection and respect for him.

Beaver agreed to come up to Oakland once again and stay until the filming of the video was completed. Beaver stayed with us for 3 weeks. He listened to the script writing and watched the filming of the role-playing. Then he narrated the sweat lodge ceremony and stated how it was used in the treatment program.

We had a big party when the video was finished. The Alameda program people were very happy with the White Cloud Lodge and New Dawn Lodge production video. Beaver received many compliments from everybody. He was like a celebrity.

The third event: In the early 1980s, there was a workshop for indigenous people who were in treatment for alcohol and other drug addictions. Seventy people—staff and clients—gathered at the Three Rivers Indian Lodge in Manteca, California. We gathered in a circle in the arbor outdoors. This was a healing circle to mend the sacred hoop that had been broken by the loss of our Native languages, ceremonies, children removed from their families and community/tribes, and many other Euro American influences.

Beaver played a key spiritual role working with the people there in the arbor. He wore his tall black hat, his silver hair flowing out beneath.

He had a gently aged, wrinkled face. His eyes showed merriment of life. He led all in a friendship dance. We not only shook hands, he showed us how to give hugs too. Beaver was adorned with his joy in life, and he shared with everybody. He had the aura of a true Indian elder spiritual leader. There was a healing energy about him. Beaver made a very positive impact.

Beaver was a Legend in His Own Time

On a personal note, Beaver and I became good friends over the years. I know him to be sincere, respectful, helpful, humorous, and full of wisdom about life. Whether while sharing a healing group, or setting up a spiritual campout, or sitting in a sweat lodge ceremony together, I always felt his healing, nurturing, and caring. I have been so blessed to know Beaver, to have been his friend, and to have been in his loving presence. Beaver was always there for others. I could call on him anytime, and he would always respond. Recently Beaver came to my home country in Montana on the Blackfeet Reservation. He was there for the Thunder Bundle opening ceremony. We got to spend a wonderful evening and a meal together. I was so glad he was there; it gave me a peaceful feeling.

Note

[1] Lobo, S. (1998). Is Urban a person or a place? Characteristics of Urban Indian country. *American Indian Culture and Research Journal, 22*, (4).

7

Helping Others Find Spirituality

Beaver continued our conversation with a discussion of his involvement with Indian spiritual practices. He provided guidelines for the correct behavior for spiritual leaders and participants in Indian ceremonies. He shared his views about the tenets of Indian religious life and the psychological challenges non-Indians and assimilated Indians experience when they become involved in these ceremonies. He admonished participants to be humble, tolerant, and forgiving. Beaver also offered his views on the proper conduct of gourd dancers and the functioning of Gourd Clan Societies.

Beaver encouraged Indian people who do not know their traditions to go back and learn them or, if this is not possible, to seek out a respected elder of another tribe. He warned against unethical ceremonial leaders who exploit those who come to them for selfish gains and gave advice on how to recognize them. He detailed the many miraculous spiritual events he witnessed in his life and offered his views on the ways of the Creator.

Beaver:

Years and years and years ago when I was young, my great uncle taught me how to run sweats, but I never did put it into practice until after I got to Three Rivers. I knew how, and I knew what the stones meant. I knew the meaning of all these things, but, matter of fact, I never anticipated, I never figured, I'd do these things, because I just didn't like people. If you didn't have a drink, I didn't want no part of you. If you wasn't somebody I could rob, steal from, and you didn't have a drink, I wouldn't have nothin' to do with you. All that has turned around.

In the beginning, in our treatment program we more or less used Alcoholics Anonymous philosophy to stay sober, but we soon realized that we needed more than that. We knew that in order to find sobriety, you had to find the Creator. At Three Rivers, there was a client. He used to come to me and say, "Beaver, can we have a sweat?" I said, "Yeah." I knew some sweat leaders. I'd get on the telephone and call 'em and ask 'em if they could come run a sweat for the residents at Three Rivers. Whenever I called they would come. At that time, anyone that came to run a sweat for our residents, we'd give 'em a hundred dollars for their effort to come down. They didn't ask it. We gave out of the goodness of our heart. We just give it to 'em to support them. This is the right thing to do. If you can afford it, it's okay for the sweat leader to accept payment, but it's not all right, it's not acceptable, to ask for or demand payment.

Those people that I kept callin' to come down and run a sweat, finally they was tellin' me, "You've got to do this. Don't be callin' all over the country to ask somebody else to come do your dirty work. You do it." Up until that time, although I really got off into the spiritual way, I wasn't ready to give up everything. I guess I wasn't really ready to make that full commitment. You have to go beyond yourself. Leading a sweat is something that most sweat leaders, most of the people I've talked to, something they don't want to do initially. More or less, the Creator has called them to do these things. They've tried and they've tried to avoid doing 'em. Eventually, they have to break down somewhere inside and make that decision to do it. There's no other way except to grow with it. If you do these things, you can't not grow. Your belief will get stronger, you'll get stronger, and your spirituality will get stronger. You'll get more often to the spiritual things than you normally would.

The more often you lead sweats, your spiritual understanding will increase.

I've had these experiences. It's not all the time that you see anything. There are certain times that you do, and it depends on where you are at in your head. I mean, not your head but with your being with the Creator. It's mainly up to Him to show you these things. I have experienced the Eagle. I've also experienced the Bear. We was up in Montana. I went to a sweat lodge. We got up there, and the bears had torn the sweat lodge, taken the covers off the sweat lodge. We put it back together, and we were settin' in the sweat lodge, prayin', and I had a vision. I seen a bear. They call 'em cinnamon bears. I seen him settin' in there next to the sweat leader, Dan. That bear was just as plain as I am sittin' here.

I seen a lotta things at the sweat lodge at Three Rivers Indian Lodge. It has a blue flame in it. Not everybody has seen that. One time our secretary came out and taken a picture of that sweat lodge. She took a picture from the door in the sweat lodge. When she had got her picture back and it was developed, that blue flame showed up in the picture. When that flame comes into that sweat lodge, if there's anybody sick in there at that particular time, they will be healed.

We had healin' in there when that flame was present, but we didn't call a healin' sweat. It just happened. The way that come about is people brought me certain things to make a smoking mixture, and I was sittin' down outside prayin', and I was mixin' my tobacco. I wasn't watching what I was putting in there. I was just lettin' Grandfather guide my hands. When I got the tobacco all fixed up, I went and burned some of it. A blue flame came out, and that kinda scared me. I said, "I'll use this in the sweat lodge tonight." That night I put some on the stones, and that blue flame came out, and everybody that was in there seen that blue flame. From that day on, when that blue flame is in that sweat lodge, somebody's gonna get healed. You don't know who it will be. It might be you, it might be someone else. The Creator knows who it will be. That flame is His way of lettin' you know that He is there and He has touched somebody.

This lady, she didn't have no kneecap. In her drunken days, she had a car wreck, and her kneecap got busted up. They had to take it out. She fell, and when she went to the doctor, they told her she probably had to go through that operation again and put some ligaments back together because it was tore loose. She's askin' me about it, and I says, "Tonight, when we go in there and pray in the sweat lodge, you sit in there by the doorway, and you pray to the Creator." When I was talkin' to her, she said, "Oh, Beaver, look at that eagle! Right up there by that treetop!" I'm lookin'. I couldn't see no eagle, but I could hear it. You know how they sound. They cry out. I heard that, and it flew away. She saw it make that circle around her, and then it flew away. She said, "The eagle's gone." I told her, "That eagle was for you to see, not for me. The Creator sent that eagle to you. He's gonna heal you tonight." That night we went into the sweat lodge. She sat there and prayed to the Creator.

When she went back to the hospital, the doctors was amazed. They said they X-rayed where they thought they were gonna have to go in and put them ligaments back together, but the problem was takin' care of itself. They was growin' back together! They said, "We never seen that before." She didn't elaborate on what was happenin', because they was kind of leery of us Indians anyway. We had a lot of healin' goin' on down there. They would never have believed her if she did tell them what happened.

I've seen a lot of healin' goin' on in that sweat lodge. I've watched it, and I've seen it done. I know it's real. I seen a woman get healed of cancer. When she went back to have her testing done, it come back negative. They was tellin' her she had to have an operation. When she went back to get her checkup and her testing, they couldn't find no trace of cancer.

Personal Remembrance

Kitty Chapman (Chuckchansi), a mother who brought her child for help

Beaver has always been a gentle and kind person, one of the most humble servants of Grandfather. I thank Grandfather for sending him into my life and the lives of my children. Beaver took me into my first sweat. He also took my 8-year-old daughter (at the time) in for a healing sweat. She did not hear well, and after being told her tonsils would have to be removed and tubes put in her ears, I called Beaver to talk with him. He said to bring her up for a healing sweat that next weekend. I did, and in the third round of the sweat, her little ears popped and drained after all the prayers and sacred songs. I took her back to the doctor on Monday morning; the doctor told me she did not need the tubes after all. Knowing Grandfather and the faith and trust I had in Him and Beaver, I knew that was what he would say. Now Beaver would be the first to say, "I am not a healer. Grandfather is." I know in my heart that if Creator had not brought me to Beaver, my life would not be what it is today. He showed me there is so much more to life than drugs, and he also showed me that forgiveness and love are the things that are of God.

Another Indian counselor at Three Rivers Lodge once objected to my helping a boy from the Tule reservation. He was thinking they should have taken care of it at Tule. I knew the boy's daddy, and his daddy knew me. He asked me if I would do it, and I told him I would. We brought him down to Three Rivers, and we went in and run a sweat for him. A healin' sweat. This other Indian counselor got real upset with it. He said I was takin' time away from the alcoholics, but I wasn't doin' that. We invited anybody who wanted to go into that healin' sweat to come in. The counselor also had a thing that we should have got permission first from the boy's tribe. He threatened to fight me on the spot to stop the ceremony, and I told him, "Okay, but you already lost." I had been a prizefighter in my youth. Luckily it didn't come to blows.

I talked to a lot of people about that one later. Even the director told me that the other counselor didn't have no business saying that about that Indian man and his kid. About a year later, I seen that man and his boy. The boy was out dancing at a powwow, and he was okay. He was close to dying before we prayed for him. Him and his daddy shook hands with me. It was worth all the BS I went through to pray for that boy.

It doesn't make no difference who comes to me for help. Anybody that needs help, needs help. I don't care what their tribe is or even if they're Indian. You help people, regardless, whether they're Indian or not. People are people. Human beins' are human beins'. I was told that. I don't understand these people that will not help a person that's not Indian. I just don't understand that.

You can also use the Gourd Clan Society to help people. Now here is what I was told about how the Gourd Clans came into existence. This tribe, they were going through a hard winter, and they ran out of food. This chief picked his most reliable warriors, and said, "You go find food for the people." They journeyed about 2 weeks and couldn't find nothing. In the morning, they heard this strange unfamiliar singing and crept up the top of this hill and looked down in the valley. They seen a red wolf dancing around a drum, and this Wolf Spirit was singing gourd songs. The spirit motioned them to come over. When they came up, he told them, "I'm going to teach you these songs and teach you the gourd dance. This is the way to the Creator." He said, "We are the Creator's helpers." He said, "When you go back, you learn these songs, learn the gourd dance, and you teach these ways to your people. Whenever they are in need, tell them to do these songs and this dance, and their needs will be supplied.

Beaver's protector, Wolf, helps those who work for the common good.

Before you go back, we will show you where you can find game, where you can find food for your people." When they went back, the Wolf Spirit told them where they could get their meat and all the food they needed. They went back, and they called all their people together and explained what the Red Wolf Spirit told them. The women cooked up a big feast and fed the warriors and the people. This is why when you see the gourd dance you thank the Creator.

Everybody gives credit to the Kiowas for bringing the gourd dance out to the open in modern times. It is debatable as to which tribe had the gourd dance first. It was suppressed a lot of years by the government because they thought it was the way of the devil. They thought we were on the warpath. Something like with the Ghost Dance. It really was meant to be a spiritual thing, making contact with God and seeking a greater understanding.

Let me tell you how a Gourd Clan Society is supposed to be. You can be a warrior, but that does not qualify you to be a gourd dancer. You have to be well respected in the community, help other people, give of yourself; then you have earned the right to be a gourd dancer. Just because you are a veteran, that does not qualify you to gourd dance. You have to earn that right by showing a better way of living. You do good for the community as a whole. When you become a society member, it makes you stronger with the Creator. It does not qualify you to be a medicine man, it does not say that you going to be a pipe carrier, it just helps you become a better human being. If you are already good, it helps you to get in better touch with the Creator. The Gourd Society gives anything that the community might need. If you're sick, you can request the Gourd Clan to come and have a ceremony for you. All you need to do is ask.

Our Gourd Clan Society often does Sun Rise Ceremonies for the community. The Sun Rise Ceremony is where we pray for you, sweat for you, especially if you are unable to do the sweat yourself. We'd do this for you. We dance the four directions for you. The Sun Rise Ceremony takes place usually at the change of the seasons. We pray for any problem that you have. We come and pray for you. We help you solve problems.

We also have what is called the auxiliary, that's women, and if you are a member of the Gourd Clan Society, that qualifies your kids, nieces, and nephews. You can bring them into the society to learn the spiritual ways. The women's role is that they take care of the cooking, sewing, and all things that people might need in that society. They help with the kids, teach them spiritual ways and what's to be expected of them, what they can and cannot do. Something like going to school. We are a family.

I don't see the women in a superior light, and I don't see them down-trodden either. I think their roles are equal as far as providing and doing these things for the society. When you take a companion, I believe that is a 50–50 deal. A woman should have the input same as the husband. If you look at it in the right context, she does a lot of work at home. I don't see the Gourd Society strictly as a men's society. The way I see this, it is a joint effort between men and women to walk a spiritual path and be closer to the Creator than they normally are and to build a foundation for their kids. The men and women are partners. Their roles complement each other. That is the Indian way.

The real heart and guts of the society, to me, is walking the spiritual path. For me myself, I see it in this light. When I am gourd dancing, when I'm at a ceremony, we're all basically human beings and we have the same feelings as other human beings. It's not "I'm better than you" or "You're better than me"; we are all equal. The basic thing is getting our lives squared with "the Man Upstairs." To me, that's the heart and guts and main emphasis.

The structure is all geared around family. In some Gourd Societies, you see little guys out there learning their spiritual way and identity with "the Man Upstairs." The warrior's main function is to be a provider who protects the old and young people and women—really, everybody in the community. The true warrior does the right thing at the right time for the right purpose. He serves the Creator. The Gourd Society, to me, is a unit of people that's working, thriving together for the good of the whole community.

The role of the warrior is often misunderstood. A true warrior is a protector and provider. Somebody that does good things for the community as a whole. Someone who got a good heart that maybe sees this grandma lady out here and gets her wood. He'll go over and help her. If she needs food, he'll share the food he's got with her. He does good things in the community to help the people as a whole. A warrior is a person that would give himself totally and will give his life to protect the people. He shares all that he's got. A warrior is the last one to take for himself. He is always concerned for the weakest ones: our kids, the elderly, someone in trouble, and those who can't do for themselves.

We don't look at him as somebody who killed somebody else. We look at it as a person who is well respected in his community, has done things for the Indian people, worked for the betterment of the Indian people. He doesn't feel he's better than they are. He treats people on an equal basis. In our Gourd Society, we'd ask someone who wants to join, "What have you done for the Indian community? Can you bring us something from your community that qualifies you to join?"

Whoever needs help, Indian or not, we made a commitment to the Creator that we would do these things: help human beings to find Him through goodness and kindness. If that White man down there, or that Mexican there, or whoever might need help came to me and said, "We need your help," I am obligated to do what I can for that human being. I made a commitment to the Creator. Before we get our gourd blankets, we build a fire inside the teepee: that's our altar. We make a commitment directly to the Creator that we are going to do these spiritual things and try to walk in a good way and help all people the best way we know how. Red, Black, Yellow, and White people and any mixture of people. We are all human beings first.

The Black Wolf Gourd Clan Society went to a D.Q. University Gourd Dance to help Dennis Banks when they were trying to extradite him and send him back to prison. We did a gourd dance for him. We asked the Creator to give him strength and help him get through this problem. We asked that he get help, that he get strength. Things worked out for him.

We go to powwows. We've been to quite a few gatherings and helped people. When we dance in the arena, we are dancing for the people—that they have a good time, a safe journey home, that everything be all right in that arena. Sometimes people come to us and ask for a special prayer. We'd do that for them.

We pray for people with physical problems and psychological problems. We pray for people with sickness. This lady we prayed for had cancer. The next time she went to the doctor, he couldn't find no trace of cancer. A lady we prayed for with claustrophobia, the next time we heard from her, she was up in Oregon running sweats. This one person we prayed for, he had some kind of infection eating on his side. It was big and round. It was eating the skin away. It was like a big old sore. It was getting bigger and bigger and bigger. The doctors told him they probably had to operate on him and cut all of it out. Our medicine was at the lodge, and I asked if we could have a ceremony for this guy, and all agreed. We had that ceremony for him, and whatever was eating at him started clearing up.

These are the type of things we've done over the years. I seen lots of things. I've seen what the Creator has done for people. I've seen good results from all these things. People get well; they get healed; they get their financial situation straightened out; some people come to us who are having problems with marriage, and years later, we find out they are still together.

Personal Remembrance

Fred Short (Chippewa), Sacramento, California, leader in American Indian Movement

I first met Beaver in the 1970s, about the time he was starting an Indian oriented alcohol treatment program in Stockton, California. At that time, I was not too interested in the traditional way or in sobriety. Beaver sensed my feelings but knew it would help me out if I got more involved in these things. Beaver told me he was getting old and could not carry some equipment around to powwows and other events. He asked me if I could help him. In this way, I got involved in spite of my mixed feelings. I realize now that Beaver was in good enough shape to carry his suitcase. He could be tricky when he wanted to be. I am now a traditional dancer and have been so for many years. Beaver was a true friend.

I was involved in the Black Wolf Gourd Clan Society when Beaver and Don Crow first started it. The society was really dedicated to helping the people. We prayed for individuals, families, and the Indian community as a whole. We prayed for the sick. We prayed for people with personal problems. We even raised money for people who needed it. Beaver and the other elders prayed constantly for renewal of the Indian community. These prayers helped bring better leadership and the community improvements that you see today. Beaver was a leader, in particular, in promoting sobriety. Beaver worked hard for community improvement but stayed out of Indian politics. He never wanted to be seen as in favor of one faction and against another.

One event that comes to mind is the help the Gourd Society gave to Dennis Banks. Dennis is a leader of the American Indian Movement, and we have worked together in AIM for many years. He was also a member of the Black Wolf Gourd Society. The state of South Dakota was trying to have Dennis extradited back there from California. South Dakota was actively persecuting AIM members, and the court system there would not have given him a fair trial and would have put him in jail. The Gourd Society prayed hard for Dennis, and the governor of California at the time, Jerry Brown, denied South Dakota's request for extradition. Our prayers were answered.

Beaver was a ready friend to all. He strongly valued the community and had a strong commitment to family life. He felt for people and went out of his way to help others. He bent over backwards to support anyone who was trying to improve himself. He was honest, straightforward, and had a lot of integrity. He told people the truth, regardless of the consequences. He was a solid person who you could rely on. He did a lot for the Indian people and for other people.

There are two kinds of Gourd Societies: the "spiritual society" and "the club." In the spiritual society, we do the things I was just talking about. We pray to the Creator, we walk the way we talk, we do these things. We do spiritual things. We believe in the Creator and in the powers of God. The club is more of a social kind of thing. They just dance. In some clubs, they even get drunk. They don't try to set an example. We have to walk our talk. We can't go out, get drunk and stagger all over the place, let our people see us or let the kids see us. We set an example for the community. This is the way it should be. If I tell you to do something, I would do it first. If I tell you to do this, it is not a thing I am not willing to do myself or have not already done. We do the right thing for the right reason.

You carry a lot of clout when you are a gourd dancer and people are looking up to you. If somebody called any member of the Gourd Clan Society, they should be willing to go and do these things for this person. To pray for them with or without a pipe. Not everyone in the Gourd Society is a pipe carrier, but everybody in the Gourd Clan Society should be spiritual enough to make contact with the Creator for another person and have enough faith in the Creator to know that this person will get whatever he is in need of.

If you were a Gourd Society member, they would call you and say, "Hey, I want you to come here to pray for me." You would be obligated to go pray for that person. You would say, "Do you want me to bring the society with me?" Either way, it's okay. Both the individual and the group are obligated to help people.

I helped start two societies, Black Wolf and Wolf Spirit. The gourd clan is a group effort. There is no such thing as independent gourd dancers. You can't freelance out there as an individual. You have to belong to a Gourd Clan Society. "Gourd Clan" and "Society" means more than one. That is the way it was explained to me. Even if you are visiting alone from a different place, you represent your Gourd Society, not just yourself. We are functioning as relatives, because we became a family.

It would not be acceptable to dance as an individual when you are away from your group unless a member of the hosting society invited you to dance at a particular gathering and the society elders approved. This has been my experience, even for a member of a society. When you go to another state or strange place, you put that blanket over your arm, you carry your fan and your rattle, and the head gourd dancer will come to you and invite you into the circle. Nowadays they got this idea going around that all you have to be is a veteran to dance, but that wasn't true in the beginning. The way I learned it, you could be a veteran and still be out there all screwed up.

When I gourd dance, I am representing the society to which I belong. People are going to look at me the way I dance, and they might make comments. When I was back in Oklahoma this last time I gourd danced, I had a regular gourd, and this old lady came up to me and said, "I see you do the right way. You have a gourd. A lot of these people use tin cans." See, that is where the Gourd Clan Society derived its name from. It's the gourd. The gourd rattles. Inside the gourd are little stones, little rocks. I was always told the best way to get those stones was to find an anthill, because those stones came from the belly of Mother Earth, way down deep. When you got them in your rattle, it gives you a certain power from Mother Earth.

If a Gourd Society falls apart or something happens to it, those members who still want to be gourd dancers must find another society and become a member of that society. If that society accepts them, okay. Depends on that society. They have to meet that society's criteria. I was taught when you walk away from the society or you're not affiliated with the society any more, you don't gourd dance until you come back or become a member of another society—unless I was invited in by existing members, and they say, "Come on. I'm going to invite you to the dance." I would feel okay about gourd dancing then. Just walking out there and gourd dancing is not acceptable.

I pray for people when they come to me and say, "I need a prayer. I need to be here and for you to pray for me." I will do that. If somebody calls me and says, "Beaver, I need you to bring the pipe to pray for me. I need prayer," I don't hesitate. I go. I don't think how I'm going to get there. I start praying 'cuz I already promised that person I'd be there, even if they are hundreds of miles away.

Let me tell you how I started carrying the sacred pipe. That started years ago. There is a secret medicine society. They started sending me lots of things. They sent them to a person in Sacramento, and he would bring them down to me. He would say, "I bring this to you to help the people." I was getting these things.

I seldom go to Native American church, but one night I got an urge. "I got to go to that church. I got to go." I went, and it was about midnight, during the water break, when this man who had been giving me things said, "There is something I got to do. This pipe was sent to me by a medicine person to give to a person here." I'm thinking, "Somebody is going to get a pipe." This guy got up and walked and got in front of me and said, "Stand up." I stood up. He says, "The medicine society sent me this pipe to give to you to help the people. These are the instructions that were given to me to give to you. You can turn this pipe down three times or you can accept it. Once you accept this pipe, that's for life. You walk with this pipe and help the people. Don't worry about where they call you to and tell you they need this pipe. Don't worry about how you going to get there or anything else about it. You just start walking and telling the Creator you're dependent on Him. He will make sure you get there. That's all you have to know and all you have to do. Everything you pray about, make sure that it comes from the Creator and that He's giving you the answers and giving you directions." Then he said, "If you ever turn around, or lose interest, or do wrong things with this pipe, make sure you take this pipe to a high mountain or high hill and face it to the east and bury it."

I got those types of calls that man spoke of, and I went trusting the Creator to provide, and He always has done so. I've done exactly what was told to me to do. I created my own ceremonies from things I seen my great uncle do. I also have songs from others. Sun dance songs, Peyote songs, Wolf songs, etc. I do this out of respect to those spirits.

This woman had a tree right by her house. She told us, "You can have this tree for wood for your sweat lodge if you don't let it fall on my house." I said, "Okay, it won't fall on your house." When my friend started sawing it down, I could have sworn it was going to fall into her house. I prayed to the Creator and said, "Please don't let this lady's house get destroyed." That's when a song came to me. For some unknown reason, I walked over and laid my hands on that tree. I sung the song, and that tree fell away from the house. I had never heard the song before, never knew it before. This is what is called "catching a song."

When we got back from the trip, we were out back cleaning up. I started to sing that song, and one of the guys said, "Beaver, I didn't know you knew how to sing peyote songs." I said, "I can't. I don't know one." He said, "You've been singing one." I said, "Was that a peyote song?" He said, "Yup." I explained to him how it come to me.

I try to do everything intertribal, because I want to respect all types. In the cities, if you go only one way, you're going to run some people off. They won't even show up, but if you stay intertribal, then they feel comfortable about coming. I caught a lot of flak. They'd say, "It should be Sioux or

Navajo, or Choctaw." There are a lot of different kinds of Indian people around here. We have to do this spiritually for all the people.

The proper way to conduct a pipe ceremony is to sit down and you really try to get to that "Man Up There." Then it all comes to you. You don't know how it will be, you really don't. You can't say it's going to be this way or it's going to be that way. You trust that "Man Upstairs," and somehow it comes together. It's like you know what you're doing, but you don't. You're just doing it.

I've used the pipe for a lot of things. Mostly to help the people find their way and help themselves. I've even prayed for people that were missing. Sometimes before the ceremony was over, there would be a call, or few days later they would show up or find out where the missing persons were at. I prayed for a woman whose husband caught a plane and went all the way down to Florida. He called her 3 days after the ceremony to tell her where he was.

I have also used the pipe to protect the people from evil. There was this wicked guy. I would call him a witch. He was harming the people. He was interfering with their spirituality. I was called and asked if I'd bring the pipe and pray for the community. I went there and prayed for the community. While I was sitting there, he come to visit with me, and he invited me over to his house. I walked into his place, and he had an altar like the one I got, only he used it in a negative way. He could point at certain things like glasses, and they would break or explode. He moved objects around. He asked me, "Can your God do that?" I told him, "He can do a lot more than that." I got a creepy feeling when I was over there. I got up and walked out, and I prayed as I walked out. I told him, "I'll pray for you." Then I went on out. I stopped and prayed for him. I knew he had power, but it was the wrong type of power.

I prayed to the Creator and asked Him to turn this man to good ways if possible. He could use it for the good of the people. In 3 days, he was dead from a heart attack. I asked God to put a lock around him to keep him from interfering with these people. God didn't turn him around, just got him out of the way. That was the Creator's decision.

You can use the pipe to heal. There was a time I prayed for this teenager who had a wreck on a motorcycle, and doctors asked his mother—they had him on life support—"Can you sign these papers so we can take him off life support?" She said, "No." Even the priest told her to do it. "There is no way this kid will be right, even if he does come off and live. He won't know what's happening. He won't even know you." She said, "I've asked this medicine man to pray for him." The priest asked her, "What did you pay?" "I didn't pay," she told him. He didn't believe her. I came and prayed for this boy that night. I knew that he was going to be all right, and he was. The people I was standing with said, "It's done. He is going to be all right." I knew it. Something just told me.

When I use a pipe for whatever reason, I sit down and pray first. I don't think there is one particular way that you pray. I think over a period of years, every time you use the pipe it is a little bit different. I don't think we have the right to pray for anything bad to happen to anyone. We turn him over to God, and He knows what that person is going to do and how he is going to do it. We leave the final decision up to Him. That guy that was evil, I asked God to have His way and His will in his life. If he was going to become a good person, that would have been okay. It was not my intention for God to take his life back. That was God's choice.

If you use this altar in the wrong way, in a negative way, negative forces have so much power down here on Earth that you can practically do anything you want. These forces are so seductive that you will be tempted to use your pipe only for evil, selfish ends. You will become the servant of evil. It is practically impossible to use it for good once you use it for evil. You must use it for the good of the people. The Creator forgives us for all our wrongs except witchcraft.

I once used the pipe to control a difficult boss. He didn't care about the residents at Three Rivers Indian Lodge, only himself. I didn't want him to get fired. We prayed that he find another job, and he got another job with more money. That's all he wanted anyway. That was the most appropriate way to remove him. I don't think I was being generous with him. It was the will of God. When I run the sweat lodge, I ask God to take all the negative things away from me that I might do or say when I'm in there. Let me be quiet. In the Bible, it says, "Vengeance is mine, sayeth the Lord." I really believe that it's not my right to take vengeance on a human being. My great-auntie used to tell me, "If you can't do something good for somebody, don't do them bad." We should act good and do the right thing, for the right reason, for the right purpose. I use the pipe not in anger but for the good of people.

When my uncle would talk to me, he'd smoke his pipe, and he'd tell me things I really didn't believe. I saw the end result of his talking with me with his pipe—the way he done it and way he said these things would come to pass. They did actually happen the way he said it was going to happen. This impressed me.

Although I've seen people get healed medically, some people would come to my uncle, and he would tell them, "I'll pray for you, but I can't heal you." He would pray for them to have less pain, but some of them he couldn't heal, and he knew that. How he knew, that I don't know. He was able to heal others. I have seen good spiritual people not get healed because the Creator is trying to build their character. I have also seen nonspiritual people get healed because the Creator wanted to build their faith and the faith of others who witnessed the healing. The outcome is the Creator's choice.

It is harder to do these things today. We don't see the great medicine people we used to see in past times. Nowadays, no Indian is entirely traditional. We don't dress as our ancestors did, except maybe when we are at a powwow or in a ceremony. We don't live in the same kind of housing as they did. Sometimes we don't even understand our languages anymore. Things have changed.

More than ever, Indian people have to be careful in what we take from the White society. We should take the good things and leave the bad. Indian people benefit from the modern conveniences—refrigerators, telephones, cars, etc.—just like everybody else. White people invented these things. We don't need the negative things from the White society, like being materialistic and hung up on your own self-interests. Keep to the traditional Indian values of generosity, humility, spirituality, and respect for all living things.

My principles, or what I learned, and the way I was raised up is what makes me who I am and where I am today. If you're a Sioux, or Kiowa, Comanche, Osage, Choctaw, or whatever tribe you are, you have to get in there and learn their culture and forget about all this other stuff that you seen on TV and all the Hollywood BS that they've put forth. Really live that Indian way, and let that become a way of life for you. Go and learn about the tribal way.

Learn the original way of your tribe. This way you'll know who and where you came from. You'll know about your ancestors. You'll know what's happened. You can educate people better that way than you can if you don't know nothin' about your own tribe.

If you have more than one tribe in you, decide where you really want to be. Do you wanna live the Sioux way? Do you wanna live the Choctaw way? Do you wanna live the Navajo way? Do you wanna live the Arapaho way? The Cheyenne way? Whichever way you pick, the one you feel that you want to become, find that tribe, and learn their way. Find an elder of that tribe that you can put a lot of confidence in, not a BSer, who will teach you that way. Do not try to learn the ways of all tribes if it confuses you. The blood is still there. Accept who you are, but focus on learning one spiritual way first. The point I am tryin' to get across is to pick the tribe with which you want to associate and focus on and become one with them, but if you do have different tribes in you, whatever tribe you're closest to, whatever tribe that you want to be like, learn their ways first.

We have a lot of ancestors out there. We don't know who's who. You can't—like with me, I can't sit here and say all my Choctaw ancestors are totally full-blood Choctaw. Who knows who they are related to 1,000 years ago? I have a lot of ancestors out there. For me to respect them all, I have to respect my ancestors from the White people too. I'm one-quarter Irish. It makes the whole person that I am. In order for you to become a whole person, you gotta respect all your ancestors and all of your spirit people. They live forever. There's no such thing as dying.

If you focus on one tribe, somewhere in there you're going to learn how to respect your other ancestry. The Creator will teach you that you should have this respect for all living creatures that He has created. It is confusing to practice the ways of more than one tribe. Get serious about one first and use that as the foundation to understanding others later.

When you're raised on the reservation or in a strong Indian community, and then you leave that environment, whether you know it or you don't, you change. You begin to change. It's altogether a different world off the reservation. You go to a city, and they don't do things like they do on the reservation. Most relocated Indian people eventually have kids. You got a lot of confused Indian kids growin' up in the big city. They don't know what's going on around them. They're so mixed up. Then, whenever they go back to the reservation, they get more confused, because it is not what they thought it was goin' to be like. You get a lotta mixed communications. What is expected from their Indian tribe doesn't make no difference in the city. That's kinda hard to balance out.

In the cities there's more tolerance to different medicine traditions. There's more tolerance to different tribal ceremonies. There's more toler-ance to different ways of dancing than there are on the reservations. If you go up in the Sioux Nation, and you bring the Miwoks in there to do their Miwok dance, they probably throw 'em out because it's not tolerated.

You gotta know who you are and what you are and accept that. I don't have no conflicts with another tribe. I'd rather see Indian people working together than to see them not working together. I know that bein' a Choctaw and knowing the background of my tribal way has helped me to be more open to other tribes.

Some of what I do is Choctaw. Some of what I do I learned from other tribal people. With a intertribal way, it is a learning process. When I first came out here to California, I looked for Indian people to associate with. I didn't like associatin' with the White folks. It is important for me not to disrespect another tribal way. I learned as much as I could about different tribes in order to show respect to those people. I think that's where a lot of us are at today. We're learnin' other tribal ways in order to show respect. Without that respect for other tribes, we got nothin'.

There are Indian tribes that have totally lost their culture. Their people want an Indian way of life. They don't want to be White. I don't blame 'em. I wouldn't want to either. If someone comes to me and says, "I want to learn about bein' an Indian," I would just have to tell 'em, "I might be able to teach you some of these things, but you have to be willing to do these things." You'd have to learn that whole way. This is a very deep subject, and it's kinda scratchy either way you go with it. There's a downside to it, and there's a upside to it. If a person really wants to be an Indian, and his tribe has lost the Indian way, he should try to find a good traditional elder of another tribe to teach him. But don't try to be everything; find one way and commit to it.

If you sun dance with a group of people, and you have accepted that as your way to talk to the Creator, that still doesn't make you of that tribe. It just makes you participatin' in a spiritual manner with them. It's very important for people to know the background of whoever they are and their people. Be clear about who you are and what you are. My being a Choctaw and being Irish, that doesn't make me more spiritual or less spiritual. I'm a gourd dancer. Now traditionally, Choctaws didn't gourd dance. It's not part of our tradition. They had Stomp dances, and they played stickball. I'm a gourd dancer. I've accepted that way as part of my spiritual path. I go that way because that's how I make my contact with the Creator. It still don't make me a Cheyenne, Arapaho, Kiowa, or Comanche. In terms of community involvement, to me, the only way urban Indians can go is intertribal. There's a mixture of all things in the urban areas.

In our Indian communities today, we have our powwow people, we have our Christian people, and we have our traditionals. I'm a big traditional. I like powwows. I like to dance. Unfortunately, I see problems with the powwows today. I don't approve of the money that has gotten into powwows. The powwow should not be commercial. The powwow is supposed to be spiritual. You're supposed to meditate and pray when you're dancing. A lot of politics has got involved into powwows. Today's powwows are not what I was raised in.

My association with Indian gatherings in my youth was strictly Choctaw, and they had one big feedin' area. You could see all kinds of pots. Big pots with food in 'em. When you got hungry, you can go and eat. Nobody charged anything. If you needed something—you'd be talking to your friend and say, "Hey, I need a horse. My old horse died on me." Pretty soon there'd be somebody come bringing a horse and say, "Here. Here's a good work horse." There was a lot of that interaction like that in the Choctaw community 60 years ago. It was more community oriented. They'd tell me, the old-timers, they used to say, "You go to these gatherings to meet old friends and to make new ones."

Everything—the way I was taught and the way I was raised—everything you do, when you're making a garment for someone, when women are making a garment for their kids, they're in prayer. When you're cooking for your family, you're in prayer. When you're dancing, you're in prayer. In the arena, when you're dancin' that circle, that's the circle of life. You pray for all the generations. Everythin' is geared around spirituality.

The right way to walk with the pipe is to judge people by who they are, not what they are. Gay Indians, two-spirits, have come to me for prayers. See, when I go to the Gay community, even when I run sweats for Gay people, what I see is that they're human beings. That's how I look at it. Everybody is a human being first. Traditional Indian people don't judge you on your sexual preference. They more or less judge you on your actions. What you're actually doing. If you're helping people, you're okay. If you're not too helpful to the people, then you're a bad person.

If a person has a dream or a vision to become a two-spirit person, he or she must obey it. That's comin' down to bein' exactly who you are and what you are and following the path the Creator has given you. If you're Lesbian or you're Gay, it's better to be who you are and what you are. Don't be ashamed. It would damage a person to do otherwise. Traditional Indians were accepting of a person, whatever their sexuality. We were fairly liberal about sex in general. Those Christian missionaries came in and turned the minds of the people on these things.

If you want to become a more accepting person, a more spiritual person, pray and meditate on what you want to be like. When you pray about it, start actin' like that person you want to be. Pretty soon you're gonna become that human bein', but it's not easy. You've got all kinds of challenges. It's a lot easier to do all the wrong things for all the wrong reasons. Do the right thing for the right reasons. If you see an old lady walking across the street, the right thing for the right reason would be to help her across the street. The reason behind that is to keep her from getting run over and killed, from getting mangled up. You don't do it expecting her to reward you or to impress others.

When you're helping other people, you're doing the will of God. The Creator wants us to help other people in order for them to have a better life. This would be a much better world if people would apply that concept in everyday livin' and do the best they know how to help someone else to overcome their problems.

You will develop your spiritual nature once you decide to live by principle. If you got good principle, even though you might offend a person, don't give up your principles. Hang with it. You cannot please everybody. Do what you think is right, and take that flak. My dad used to say, "Let the chips fall where they may."

To be who I am and what I am today, I totally had to turn my will and my life over to God the way that I understood him. I know a lot of people don't understand God the way the general population does out there. I do know they understand God in their own way. To me, it's important to find what God is to you and just turn your will and your life over to the Creator and totally follow that, come what may. You just follow the will of God. It might offend a lot of people. It might cause you to have problems in your own life, with your companion. If you really truly believe that is the will of God, you do it.

I was married to a Sioux woman, and she couldn't follow these ways. She couldn't be spiritual. We had to go our separate ways. We had a good understanding on that. We talked about it. She chose to go back to drinking, and I chose to go on with this life I've got. I told her, "If I lose my sobriety, I'll lose my livelihood, I'll lose my home, I'll lose my spirituality, and I'll lose you. I will have lost all the way round. But by letting you go, I'll just lose one thing: you."

Whenever somebody asks me to do something for 'em, whether it be healing, finding somebody, or whatever it might be, I sit down and pray first. I turn my whole self over to God and the way that I understand Him. I ask Him if it's His will and His way that I should go and do these things for these people. I pray, "Make the way." To this day, He has always provided a way and means. One thing I know that really, really helped me is the prayers that my family put down to God. They prayed for me all the time.

Opportunities come 'round all the time when you ask the Creator. You don't really know where they're comin' from or anything about it. When you sit down and pray, for whatever reason, make sure it's a need. Just ask for your needs. Us human beings can turn a want into a need. We can turn up a lot of different ways why we need this and why we need that, but basically it is often just a want. I ask the Creator in this way: "If it's a need, you know my needs before I ask you. If it's a need, send it to me." I ask Him to have His will and His way in my life in all things that He gives me.

One time I needed 50 dollars. Fifty-two dollars and something cents. I sat down and prayed, "Grandfather, send me what I need, and you know what it's for." I got a check in the mail for the very same amount that I needed. It was right to the penny that I needed. For me, that was awesome! God will take care of you if you give Him a chance. When you pray, go away expecting good things to happen, and it will come to pass that way. At least it always has with me. God is not a respecter of individuals. What He has done for me He will do for you or anyone else. Sometimes God will grant you your wants. I call them my fringe benefits.

Sometimes you tell the Creator exactly what you need, and you put it down pretty plain: "Grant me my needs. Not my wants." If it's a want, the Creator always knows that. If it's just a want, and it don't come about, that's okay. You feel good in yourself even though it didn't happen. We don't know the will of God. We don't know how far He sees down the road. He sees further down the road than we do. He knows when what we're asking for is not the right thing for us. Maybe He has a better solution for us. Chances are He'll bring that one about. Once I prayed to be able to buy the land Three Rivers Indian Lodge is located on. I thought it'd be better than continuing to rent. God did not grant that prayer. Later, I came to learn of some problems with buying this land. We would have lost our program if we had bought the land. God knew this.

If you want to become a more spiritual person, you should stay humble. That's easier to do if you stay out of Indian politics. We get kind of squirrelly. We get crazy in the head. I've seen a lot of good people go the other way on account of politics. Some Indian people will hurt the interest of the community as a whole through their political ego or their wants. They forget about the people. I used to say 50 years ago that the Black people were going to advance quicker than the Indian people because they were willing to work together for the good of the group. Then they was the bottom of the financial pile. Nobody believed me, but time has shown I was right.

Before you go in to have your community meetings, the board meetings, or tribal meetings, sit down and pray and ask God to be with you and to keep you humble. Always remember who you are. You're just a human bein'. Go ahead and state your views and opinions. If it goes, it goes. If it don't, if they throw you out, they throw you out. Let it roll off you like water off a duck's back.

With other people in these meetings, have compassion for 'em. Try to forgive them when they oppose you. They're just human beins'. They're doing what they think they really should be doin'. Whether it is right, wrong, or indifferent. Try to put yourself in their position and in their place. Sometimes people are squirrelly because they don't know no better. Try to hang in there. Don't give up too quickly on an organization. We Indian people tend to walk away too soon when we get frustrated. On the other hand, if you try hard to get a group to see it when they are doing something wrong, there does come a point when you must leave—if they don't change their ways—otherwise, people will think you support what that group is doing. Pray hard, before making that break, for guidance.

Never give up on a person as long as that person's got breath. If he's breathing, he's still got a chance to be a better human being. The same way with alcohol and drugs. That was basically one of the first things I learned. Don't give up on a human being as long as they're breathing. They have a chance to turn it all the way around. That is quite true.

It's not what you've been or what you come from that makes you a good person. You could become a good human bein' even if you was the worst human bein' before you turned your life around. I used to tell the residents of Three Rivers Indian Lodge, even Charles Manson has a chance to live a good life. All he's gotta do is turn his will and his life over to God the way he understands Him. He too can have that chance.

We're so quick to judge a human bein' and to condemn them for what they do. I think if we could understand his motivation for doing what he's done, we could help him overcome a lot of that anger, a lot of that bad feeling that he has. The hard times we have had in our life build character. I would not be who I am today if I had not had some tough times and learned from them.

When you are going through hard times, it is just like when you are in the sweat. It might be so hot you don't think you're goin' to make it, but you know that flap is goin' to be raised soon, and you'll cool off. The best way is to keep prayin' until that flap comes up, knowin' things are going to ease. Do the same in difficult times. Keep praying. God will see you through 'til the easier times, and you will be purified in the process.

Be careful who you choose as a spiritual teacher. Most people that have been workin' in the Indian community, a pipe carrier or a spiritual leader, their reputation will generally speak for itself. Main thing you should know is his name. If he's who he says he is, then you can go with that one. A lot of times you don't know if that person is right, wrong, or indifferent. Anyway, if you have that feelin' not to trust that human bein', don't!

In picking a teacher, it's not so much how he presents himself, both good and bad. Some people present themselves in a good way, and it might be bad with some other people. It might be good to other people. Go by your own feelings. Pray when you go to meet that person. Pray about it. You'll know if you have good feelins' or if you have bad feelins'. Those feelins' will be there if you trust in the Creator.

Don't worry about phony medicine people. If you're walking with the Creator, He will let you know that those people are not of Him and that the spirit that they got is not the spirit of the Creator. You get a funny feeling. You have to experience it to know it. I can't explain it; it's unexplainable. It's just something that you will feel if you practice these spiritual things.

Generally, when a medicine person comes to you, they should not be looking for monetary things. If they quote you a price, then you run in the opposite direction from which they came. We do these things for the people, not for the money. Money has no place in what you do spiritually for the people. If you need money, or if you need anything, and your heart is in the right place, and you're doin' the right things for the right reason and the right purpose, God is going to supply that need for you. A true medicine person doesn't look for money. He doesn't need to become a beggar and beg for money. He doesn't need to do any of those things.

I've seen bad things done by medicine people. I've watched them do it. I knew it wasn't right. I knew they wasn't doin' the right things, but I wasn't in no position to correct 'em because I wasn't doin' no better myself. That was before I started walking the spiritual way. After I started walkin' the spiritual way, if I see it done, I have the authority to correct 'em and say, "You shouldn't do that. You shouldn't be doin' it this way. You should be doin' it the way the Creator gave it to you."

I have seen medicine men who have gotten sexually involved with people they were supposed to help. It happens all the time. You gotta really know that person that was seduced, and you gotta know that medicine man. A lotta times these people could avoid that one if they really wanted to avoid it. I'm not saying it's right, I'm just saying it's avoidable. There is a boundary; you can get only so close. You can't get too close. There's a line that you draw. It's an invisible line. You get to the point of being close to that person, but you don't step over that line to taking advantage of them. You should have no unnecessary interaction with the person that you're trying to help. I can't go into detail. Some people might think anything would be over the line. Others of 'em might have a broader view about what they would consider over the line. Use your own conscience, your own moral standards. Use them and let them be your guide.

A real spiritual pipe carrier would say the same thing I'm saying. You don't cross that line. If you come to a person for help, his primary purpose is to help you to find God. It is wrong to take advantage of those who come to you in need. You treat them like a sister or brother. You do the best you know how for that person. You let it go at that. I hope that I always do the right thing for the right reason and for the right purpose: to help that human bein' find God and find joy.

Turn your will and your life over to God the way you understand Him. He's going to take care of you. Commit yourself into His hands. What belongs to God, God takes care of. When you said, "I'm going to walk with you, Creator," that means if you really, really mean it, you will do these things, because you want to live a good spiritual life. You want to do those things pleasing to the Creator. The less you do to please yourself, the more benefits you're going to get from the Creator.

Participating in sweat lodge ceremonies can help your spiritual development. For whatever purpose you go there, you should go in there humble. Not "I'm better than this person, I'm better than that person." Just go in there as a human bein' accepting something from the Creator and expectin' to receive whatever you go in there for. When I run a sweat, I always tell 'em, "If you don't get what you come in here for, then you better check your spirituality. You better make sure that you come in the right way. If you got any hate or any animosity in yourself towards another human being, that first round is for every individual to pray for themselves and to get rid of that bad feeling."

A person that's leading a sweat should have high morals and be respected by his peers. Not looked up to, but be respected by his peers. If you put a person too high on a pedestal, it won't be long before he's got stones thrown at him tryin' to knock him off. He must be humble and fair-minded. He should not take sides in the community.

The way the Indian people look at the sweat lodge, it is the womb of Mother Earth. When we come out of there, we're just like a newborn baby. All the garbage that we went in there with, we leave with the stones. We send 'em to the Creator that way. When we leave there, we're just like that innocent baby that was just born. We got no animosity. We got no hate. If we die at that particular time, we're okay. Probably the cleanest we'll ever be. That is, if we can make that contact with the Creator and leave all these difficult things there with the stone people.

If people who come into the sweat are angry at each other, they really should talk to the sweat leader and say, "I don't like that guy over there. What should I do?" That sweat leader should consider it, and if he thinks he can work it out with 'em in the sweat lodge, then he should bring 'em in and work it out for 'em. If he thinks it's going to cause a problem within the lodge, within the group, he should ask them to leave. He's responsible for all those other people in that lodge. He should offer to sweat with just the two of them if they want to make peace.

A sweat leader can have a special ceremony for people who are upset with each other and want to reconcile. Sometimes it's good for the leader to be polite, and sometimes you have to hit 'em over the head with the nitty-gritty. Get their attention and get them to do a self-inventory. Tell them that in order to grow spiritually, they have to be forgiving. Never bring quarreling people into a general sweat. If you've got these bad vibes going in, it's bound to rub off onto other people. With two people that got animosity towards one another, if they're sitting in a ceremony to pray, think about the conflict those two people are going to cause for everybody sittin' in there. It's the same principle. That's why the medicine man, he tries to get rid of those bad vibes by brushin' 'em off with an eagle feather or putting water on 'em.

The leader of a spiritual ceremony should make every effort to put any bad feelings toward another participant away and try to make that person feel worthwhile. If you cannot leave your problems back home or wherever it happened, you should stay out. It didn't happen there, so don't bring it there. The sweat leader shouldn't show up at the ceremony with animosity and hard feelings. This also goes for everybody involved with running that sweat. Gene, you told me how you went to one of my sweats and had a bad experience with a fire keeper. You said he was mad at you about something from outside and kept glaring at you. If I had known at the time, I would have told him he shouldn't be carrying those stones if he can't forgive and let go of things. He was there to be of service and help everyone present feel better about themselves and get closer to the Creator.

When you're running a sweat, you try to do it for the people, not just for yourself. As a sweat leader, you should have enough confidence in yourself with the Creator to know that "I'm with the Creator and nothing can touch me. If it does, that's okay too, because I'm gonna be with the Creator." For me, myself, I would sweat if the devil come to me and said, "Beaver, can you take me into a sweat lodge?" I'd say, "It might just be me and you, but I'll take 'ya in." I know the Creator will protect me.

Sherry Atkins (Apache), Merced, California, sweat lodge leader

I first met Beaver in 1983 at a sweat ceremony. Beaver, or "Grandpa Beav," as we call him, at that time was a counselor at White Cloud, in Oakland. He also ran sweat ceremonies at Three Rivers Lodge. He was a member of Black Wolf Gourd Society.

He was a traditional war dancer and member of a local powwow committee. Beaver was always going somewhere to help someone. He was a very kind and gentle man, speaking words of wisdom, always patient and soft-spoken. He treated everyone well, no matter how they might act. He would say, "If an individual is having a hard time or being negative, pray for them. Always say a good word, and when you speak, keep it simple, and be willing to walk the path Creator puts in front of you." As I see it, this was Beaver's philosophy of life. Beaver has been an inspiration to me to this day. Just watching him and listening to him has been a great support for my family.

I have seen Beaver put his teachings about patience into action. I remember one time we were at a sweat and these guys showed up. There were four of them sitting in a van drinking alcohol before the ceremony. Beaver was setting the fire, but he knew what those guys were doing. He never said anything to them. So I said, "Beaver, those guys have alcohol over there. Don't you think we should put them off the grounds?" They were a rough-looking bunch, too; they had White Power tattoos, shaved heads, Nazi symbols on their van, skin, and clothes. To me, they didn't seem very friendly. Beaver reminded me, "The sweat lodge is where people come to get well, a place of healing."

Two of those guys went into the lodge. When Beaver asked them to introduce themselves, they said nothing. He asked them if they had ever sweated before. They still wouldn't answer. Finally, Beaver said to them, "This is going to be a very hot sweat, and for this special ceremony I don't want anyone to break the circle by leaving." The door to the sweat was still open, and one of the newcomers looked over at Grandpa and said, "It can't get too hot in here for me. I know I can take it, and if this is about race, and you don't want me in here because I'm White, then just say so." Then he proceeded to smack his own chest with his fist. Beaver told the doorman to close the flap.

On the first round, those guys started to moan and move around a little. By the second round, they started crying. Then one guy started hysterically yelling, "Tell them your name, Tommy! Just tell them your name!" Then they said, "We're taking medication! It's the kind of medicine that you can die if your body temperature gets too high!" When the door opened on the third round, one guy was lying faced down, crying. The other was sitting cross-legged, rocking back and forth, also crying (this was the one with the smart mouth). Their tattoos were all sweated off. They said, "Grandpa, please let us out! We are going to die in here!" Grandpa Beaver looked at them for a long time and said, "I can't think of a better place to die than the sweat lodge."

When the sweat was over, those guys took off running so fast they left their shoes behind! Their friends in the van had already left, so those guys kept on running all the way to the main road! About 3 years later, the one guy named Tommy came back. He looked entirely different; also, his attitude was much improved. Tommy told us two of his friends from that sweat were now dead, the other one was on death row, and that he had spent 2 years in prison. Tommy also shared that during his time in prison he thought about and remembered a lot about his experience in the ceremony. He said he believed he had found something very special and it had changed his life for the better.

My great uncle did a lot of things. He had his teachings from the kwa-nokashas, and they taught him all the things he knew. They taught him, among other things, how to take people on vision quests. He'd tell 'em, "If you want to find God, this is the time. This is your time alone with God." The vision quest is a one-on-one, you and God. This is the time that you don't have to worry about people, places, and things, because this is your time alone with God. The Creator sends his helpers at these times to give you information.

The Earth is our mother. We came from the Earth. Everything we use is from the Earth. Nature itself works hand in hand with the Creator. You can't have one without the other. Man can duplicate a lot of things, but he can't duplicate what Mother Nature has here, like the trees, the grass. We've got the four seasons: winter, spring, summer, and fall. Our cars, our furniture, everything that we have came from Mother Earth. The materials we used in making these things, the Creator gave man knowledge of how to use 'em, how to put things together. He gave us that knowledge of how to do certain things.

God and Nature is one and the same. When I look at the trees and I look at the grass, it reassures me that God is real. Who could make a tree? Who could make a leaf? Who could do these things? There's gotta be a Creator somewhere that started all of this in the beginning. That's where I am with that one. Nature and Spirit. On a vision quest, you might see a bear. Spirits come to you. You might see a wolf, a bird, or an ant. God uses Nature to send you a message.

Recently, I saw a wolf and a bear when we was building the sweat lodge for a vision quest. When they was putting the sweat lodge together, I was sittin' in the camp area. I looked up, and I seen, in the road, this wolf and this bear sittin' there looking at me. I thought my eyesight was playing tricks on me. I shook my head and rubbed my eyes and looked again. They was still there. I got up to go down and tell the guy that was building the sweat lodge, "Come up and see the wolf and the bear." When I got up, they just disappeared. Yeah, and I knew what it was. I knew it was a vision. Wolf and Bear were there to protect those people.

The Indian experiences God through Nature. It's so simple yet it's a complex situation; maybe you have to be an Indian to understand? I don't know. For me, I don't question God. Only thing I know is that He does exist and that He existed long before we as human beings was here. He exists in Nature. He surrounds all things. He lives in all things. He is a divine force that can be called upon for help.

Sometimes nature spirits, God's helpers, just show up when you need them. About 25 years ago, I was in a bad car wreck. My car was hit by a truck that ran a stop sign. It all happened so fast that I didn't have time to react. My life flashed through my mind. I started thinking of all the things I had done in my lifetime. It was just the way people say it happens before you are going to die. I thought, "This is it; I'm gonna die."

A few seconds before that truck hit me, three wolves appeared on the car's hood—a red wolf, a black wolf, and a white wolf. They sat and looked at me. I knew the Creator had sent them to protect me and I was going to be all right. The car was crushed like an accordion. The fire department had to cut me out of my car. Everybody there was amazed that I was not dead. I didn't have a scratch on me. They took me to the hospital, and the doctors were amazed. They told me people usually died or were badly injured in the kind of accident I had. I was not hurt. I was not even sore.

When you're putting a person on the hill to seek a vision, your job is to pray every day for that man or woman. Whoever it might be. You're totally responsible for that person. You run a sweat for that person. You make sure that everyone who is there is focused on the person(s) on the hill and praying that they will receive/see the vision that they've come there for. You say prayers for those on the hill. If I put somebody on a hill, I wouldn't feel comfortable in going off and leaving 'em up on a hill and coming back later. The leaders should stay there the whole time. Some people understand their vision before they come down. It'll come to some other people during the time they're talking to me after they've come down. I try to help them understand it.

I would like to say something about the place of non-Indians in our ceremonies. In order to keep the Indian philosophy and the Indian way growing, you gotta keep the majority of participants Indians. I would say it applies in general, even with sweats. This is so that we have that impact as Indians. It is okay to allow non-Indians to participate, but they should be in the minority.

I have seen some Indian spiritual leaders who have ceremonies where most of the participants are White. I think these leaders are phonies. I don't think they're telling it like it really is. I think they're not being truthful with the people in the sweat lodge with them or about what they're doin'. My experience with Indian people, if you're not really doing what you say you're doing, Indian people will leave you high and dry, and all you got left is the non-Indians. I've seen it over and over and over. The best way to have an all-White Indian organization or have an all-White sweat is to start getting crazy. Follow the traditional way. Be fair, honest, and humble. Keep things Indian; it has to be that way!

Many non-Indians experience culture clash when they go to our ceremonies. The time issue is a good example of that one. See, in the Indian world, we don't have time. In ceremonies, there's no clocks, nothing like that. When it's time to be there, you be there. When it's not time to be there, you're just not there. You don't tell a person, "Hey, you got this amount of time to do this and that amount of time to do that." You don't put things on a time frame. A lot of non-Indians can't handle that one. It's gotta be on a time frame for them to be comfortable.

We've had 'em come, and they say, "Well, what time you gonna start?" We tell 'em; we estimate a time. We get there, and maybe it didn't happen at that time, and they'd ask me, "Well, when do you really start?" I say, "When those stones get ready, they'll tell you. We'll go in when the stones are ready. You see that man over there with the pitchfork? He's the fireman. He'll let you know when the stones are ready." They ask, "Well, how does he know?" I says, "When they get red-hot, he'll let you know." It is not by time but when it's ready; when you feel it's ready.

A lot of assimilated Indians are in the same boat because they was put on a time frame in school or somewhere on the job. The non-Indian society is all about time. If they're gonna go back to their roots, they have to forget about time. They gotta get to the point where they can accept this Indian way, that don't got no sense of time, without feeling bad.

Most of the White people I've run across has a disbelief about our spiritual way and about our medicine. They don't believe in the spirit world. They have a hard time really acceptin' the Indian belief system. It is different than the American belief system.

Now, even some Indians have a hard time with our traditional beliefs. Since the White man came over, I guess we've been going through a change in our culture and beliefs. This is the question: Can you do it the traditional Indian way? If you believe in these Indian ways, I will talk to you about spiritual things and what I've seen. If you don't believe in these ways, I might not say very much to you.

There was this Indian man who was a resident at Three Rivers Lodge. He was always criticizing our Indian spiritual ways. He was real negative. He said we was old-fashioned and that modern-day Indians did not believe in these things anymore. He was saying all this one day as we was building a fire for the sweat lodge. All of a sudden, fire jumped from the fire pit and burned the man's arm. He was standing over 10 feet away from the fire! There was not a strong wind or anybody stoking that fire before he got burnt. This made him a believer. He became a sweat lodge leader and has been running sweats for many years up in Oregon.

You see, Fire has a spirit—just like the other elements of Earth, Wind, and Water. These powers know what you are thinking. You must be respectful towards these powers or you could get harmed. When you approach these elements, talk to them in a good way. When you build a sweat lodge fire, tell the fire that your intention is to heat stones in order to help the people. Then everything will go well.

Indians are hesitant about telling people what they have seen and what has happened because of the unbelief coming from their listeners. My experience with that one is, the best thing to do is to say nothing about it, because they have an ego problem. They either think you're ignorant, or they think you're phony. There's a lotta things that I've seen and I know. Only way I'll share these things is with someone that I really know believes these things can happen and that they have happened.

Indians go to the source, and the source is the Creator. With the non-Indian, they write everything down. Maybe their writing is true, and maybe it's not. You have no way of checking references on this one. Some of 'em wouldn't accept a spiritual event even though the experience hit 'em in the face. I've seen people that way—the experience has actually been there, and it happened to them and for them, but yet they couldn't accept the fact that that came from the Creator.

The whole understanding of life of a traditional Indian has been taught around these things. Their grandmas and their grandpas or aunts and uncles has talked about these things. They've seen it! They know it happens, and they got more influence on the kids, tellin' 'em, "Hey, I've seen this. This is the way it was." They have learned to be humble about these things.

Sometimes Whites who get involved in Indian ceremonies want to take it out of the concept that it's really meant to be. Some use it as an authority-type thing. This is not about authority. Some of them start to want people to admire them if they help out at a ceremony. They even get bossy. It's supposed to be more of a sharing-type thing. Our whole Indian culture is based on giving, being a servant to others. My great uncle, medicine man, was a very giving type of person. He always told me, "This don't belong to us. It belongs to God. He let us use it for a period of time. It belongs to the Creator."

Some of our modern-day Indians, they like a name and title. It seems like they forget who they are and what they are and who they're supposed to help. I see that a lot. A lot of times, the non-traditional Indians, if you give 'em a title or start looking up to 'em as a good helper, they also use it in the wrong way. Their ego gets in their way. They think, "I'm somebody in the Indian community." The Indian people are thinking, "They're nobody in this community."

I seen that happen to a lot of Indian people. They become a pipe carrier, and our community starts looking up to him as a spiritual leader, and then they get the big head. Pretty soon they're doing things, and they're causing a lot of divisive, bad feelings in the community. It just makes for a bad situation. With the Indian people, you've gotta be very careful, or they'll leave you sittin' high and dry. You've got to be the humble servant of the people, or else what good are you?

If you become a ceremonial leader, be honest about your shortcomings. People are people, and they're gonna look for your flaws. Once they find 'em, they gonna rip you to shreds if you pretend to be perfect. We all have flaws, but when you catch 'em, make sure that you're up front with 'em and say, "Hey, I'm not a perfect human bein'." If you tell people you're a perfect human being, they're gonna sit there and study you until they know you real good. They're gonna find something wrong and tear you apart. You gotta admit your short comings. Be honest about it.

There are some good medicine people who are a little crazy. If they want to be social, I'll socialize with 'em. If they want to be left alone, I'll leave 'em alone. It depends on that person. Being a medicine man, you're bound to be a little crazy. You have to be a little bit off your rocker to do these things, and some of the things you experience make you a little crazy. The true medicine person does not really have a choice. They were born to be medicine people.

All the medicine people, they didn't do it all right away. Some of them taken years, 4 or 5 years, to get ready to do these things. Most of 'em kind of lived their wild and wooly life for a while. I think that was a transition they had to go through in order to get prepared to do what they was born to do. That transition to doing what they was supposed to do kind of made 'em a little nutty. If I am around a medicine person who seems a little off balance, I ask God to have His will and His way with this person. That's doctorin'. I pray that the Creator will help them to do what they're supposed to do.

I have attended a few Peyote Ceremonies. I respect the Peyote Way, but I don't have too much to say on it because I don't understand Peyote that good. Only thing I know, it has helped people. I'm that way about all religions. If it helps you, that is good. As for myself, I don't want to be influenced by chemicals, and I don't want to receive visions by chemicals. I'd rather just sit down and pray with my pipe and get a understanding with God or go on a vision quest and fast, pray, and meditate.

I don't understand Indians who claim they are traditional but say they are Christians. Christianity is not a traditional Indian religion, but I support anything that's good for the people and that's gonna benefit another human bein'. I don't have no bad feelings about doin' these things to help people, whether it be peyote or sun dance or gourd dance or whatever. Even the Christian way. Man created religions. God created the spiritual way. Follow the spiritual path that gets you closest to God.

The traditional Indian way is to get close to those helpers the Creator has assigned to us. Everyone has a spirit guide. I believe that. When you're around ceremonies, it's not always that you could call 'em; they just come when they know that you need some information or whatever. They'll come to you and give you whatever it is that you need. The way they let you know that they're around, a lot of times they'll move things on you.

They'll move your furniture around, move your stuff around, or move something around to let you know that they been there. Sometimes they will show up as lights. It's funny how these spirits will work.

Personal Remembrance

Pete Bacca (Comanche), Squaw Valley, California, ceremonial leader

I first met Beaver in 1992 when I was invited to attend a meeting of the Black Wolf Gourd Society. I joined the society a year later. Beaver was my sponsor during the initiation phase. Differences of opinion developed over how the society should function. Some of the members, under Beaver's leadership, decided to break off and start a new society. This is how the Wolf Spirit Gourd Society began.

Beaver put me up on the hill several times. I received powerful visions and medicine. One time, the bear came to me. On another occasion, I had a powerful vision of the wolf. The wolf gave me a song that I use to help others. The wolf is my spirit helper. I am now a wolf dancer. I call on the Wolf Spirit when I lead sweat lodges. I have come to understand over the years that the wolf medicine is love. The wolf pack is tied together by love and affection.

Beaver possesses the wolf nature. He sits and carefully observes. He is not rough like the bear people. He chooses his moment to act. He always has in mind the good of the group. He gets the group to work as an efficient team. If any individual becomes selfish and forgets the group good, Beaver is that lead alpha male who nips at them until they are back in harmony with the group. He is patient, affectionate, resourceful, and forceful.

Beaver has helped me greatly increase my spiritual awareness. I am better able to see what is coming. I see more clearly other people's nature. Beaver and I have conducted sweat lodge ceremonies together in which we were able to communicate telepathically. We spoke without words or sound. He has helped me to become calmer and more focused.

Beaver came to sweat with women I worked with in state prison. It was moving to see how hardened individuals softened up in his presence. The women really loved Beaver. Today, some of them attribute their better attitude toward life to having met him. People were always drawn to Beaver whenever we would set up the Gourd Society Teepee. People would come to visit with Beaver for hours. They loved speaking with him, even very traditional tribal people at ceremonies like the Bear Dance.

Beaver has taught me many things. I am a better person for having known him. I have better relationships with friends and family and work harder for the good of the people. I am more patient and loving than I used to be. I have been really touched by that old man. The greatest gift he has given me is the knowledge that it is possible to be a traditional Indian in the world today.

When I pray to help someone, spirits come and do the work. I don't want to take credit for something that they do. They are the Creator's helpers. When you're prayin' for people, you call in the spirits, and you can feel their presence. When you feel the spirits and feel their presence, you know something positive is going to get done. You just turn it over to them. You're more or less just there. They're the ones that's doin' the work. That's why I said I didn't want to take no credit for what they have done. You can't get away from your spirit helpers. You can't get away from that spiritual entity. If you go to New York, they will be there.

Somehow you just know that they're there, and you get a feelin'. You feel 'em there. Sometimes you hear or see them. There is a set of helpers who come to me, but different ones show up for different needs. It depends on what I am praying for. I have found that sometimes if you're prayin' for a person to get well of a certain disease, there is a spirit that comes that will help you with that one. If you're prayin' for something else, like a lost person, there's another spirit that will come help you with that one. Go to the source, the Creator, and pray. He will send you the helpers you need, or the problem may just go away.

I know the soul exists independently of the body. I've been up there lookin' down on my body. After we die, I think our spirits go to a place that's a lot better than this one. I don't think a person really dies outright. I think when you have crossed over, you leave what you have done in this life and what you have taught people. It goes on and on and on and on and on and on and on. Whatever is good about us stays. Whatever we might be able to teach another human bein' just stays. It keeps going.

I was talking to one of my relatives one day. We was reminiscing 'bout the ole days. She told me, she says, "God brought you through all of that." She said, "It's a wonder you hadn't got killed when you were growin' up in your younger years." She never thought I'd become a spiritual person.

Some people who knew me in those years were really surprised when I changed. I went from trying to settle disputes with my fists or a gun to trying to see the other person's point of view and do what I could to help them. I turned my life and will over to the Creator. Do that one.

I was crazy. I was wild and crazy. I began to start looking inside and to stop running away with my feet or by doing drugs and alcohol. I learned to do that "self-inventory." I look back at the way I was and the way I am today. What you see right now, the way I am right now, and the way I was 40 years ago, you wouldn't believe that I'm the same person. It's like turnin' a light off and on. That is the difference. The difference is much like daylight and dark. When God turned me around, He turned me around.

Whenever you have a problem, turn it over to the Creator. He sees way down the road and will give you what you need. When you pray and turn a problem over to that "Man Upstairs," stop worrying. When you worry, you take the problem back. Pray for faith if it is lacking. After you pray, go away knowing good things are going to happen for you.

What I have said and what I have done, these are truly not only my words. It was spoken years and years before me. Someone else has said the very same thing, maybe in a different context or a different light or slightly different way. Maybe they got the point across better than I did, but the meaning is the same.

Note

1 Brown, L. (1997). *Two Spirit People*. New York, NY: Harrington Park Press.

8

Conclusion and Discussion

There are in actuality two stories in this document: 1) an Indian man's having a difficult start in life that led to substance abuse and a life of crime, and that same man developing a very warm, giving, self-confident approach to life in his middle years and later life that not only led to his transforming his own life but also helped him promote positive changes in the Indian community; and 2) the spiritual teachings of a respected American Indian elder. Beaver's life is an inspiration.

Beaver has been open and honest with us. He tells us he lost his mother as a boy, suffered abuse in a racist Indian boarding school, faced mortal combat in World War II, and lost contact with his beloved children after the stormy end of his first marriage. He says that he coped with these traumas for many years by impulsive, violent, acting-out behavior and self-medicating with drugs and alcohol. He is humble in the way he relates these things. Given the depths of his pain and anger, it is miraculous that he turned his life around and became a positive individual.

The key to Beaver's success appears to be that he did not see "recovery" as just for himself. He knew the Indian community as a whole needed recovery. He worked for over 40 years to improve the quality of Indian family and community life. As a true warrior, Beaver sought to protect the weakest ones, the children, and encouraged others to remember the needs of Indian children by committing to clean and sober community events.

How can we account for the dramatic shift in Beaver's life? First, and most important, is his self-confident approach to turning his life around—*he believed he could change his life if he tried.* Secondly, he decided to develop altruistic social relationships. This was no small achievement, given his rage at how he was treated in an Indian boarding school, his anti-social lifestyle, and his general dislike for people. Fortunately, he returned to the childhood teachings of his beloved medicine man uncle and thereby reclaimed traditional Indian spiritual values.

In a past investigation, I demonstrated that precisely these three things—the self-confidence to try to improve one's life, the willingness to take risks and develop better social relationships, and defining a clear value system—are associated with overcoming difficult childhood environments and developing positive mental health in adulthood.[1] Other psychologists have found similar associations for self-confidence,[2] altruism,[3] a clear value system,[4] and subsequent positive mental health. Beaver acknowledges his personal commitment to turning his life around and the good foundation he received from the Choctaw community of his early childhood. Beaver himself gives most credit for his recovery to the prayers of his relatives and his turning his life over to the Creator.

What are the key features of Beaver's teachings? He argues that anyone can turn his/her life around if he/she is honest about who he/she is and is willing to "be themselves," do what is right, and take whatever flak comes. He states that we must accept and help others—simply because they are human beings. He reminds us to judge others by "who they are, not what they are." We are, in his opinion, "our brother's and sister's helper," and we should care for one another's well-being. He urges Indian people to learn and respect their own tribal traditions and values and to work together intertribally for the good of all Indians. While urging Indian people to work for the greater good of the community, he emphasizes that we must avoid the pitfalls of "Indian politics" by remaining humble. He says leaders must unite the people, not divide them by using manipulating issues such as blood quantum or enrollment status. In the recent movie *Doe Boy*, a traditional Indian elder speaks these cogent lines after a deer hunt: "Nobody cares how much blood a deer has, but everybody wants to know how much blood an Indian has." To Beaver, whether light- or dark-skinned, we are all Indians and should remember that. He recommends that Indian people work together for the good of the whole community.

Beaver's call for Indians to return to traditions is timely and important. The 2010 U.S. census indicates that the number of individuals claiming to be American Indians has greatly increased. Surely part of this phenomenon is explained as the reclaiming of Indian ancestry. Euro American families in particular have historically downplayed or denied familial ties to what was considered a socially inferior people.[5] Further, the indigenous roots of Mexican

American culture are once again being honored.[6] We see greater involvement of Chicanos in American Indian powwows and the revival of Aztec dance forms. Some Black people are increasingly rejecting the "one-drop rule" of American racism, which holds that if you are any part Black, you are only Black. We see the rise of Black American Indian organizations today and the resurgence of the Black Indian identity.[7] A renowned African American psychologist once told me that it was important for African Americans to reclaim their links to American Indians. Many African Americans have family oral histories of long-ago Indian ancestors.

This process of reclaiming a discarded Indian identity is better referred to as "ethnic renewal" and subsequent engagement in the Indian community as "retraditionalization."[8] The demographics of the modern-day Indian community will be further complicated in the future by the fact that more than half of enrolled Indians are married to non-Indians. This may be creating identity challenges for offspring of these unions who choose to be actively involved in the Indian community. This has been true for mixed-bloods since earliest contact.[9] Beaver was keenly aware of these issues for urban Indians and felt counselors of American Indians needed to adopt a very open and inclusive attitude.

Some Indian tribes have lost their traditions and are actively renewing ceremonies.[10] Indian people in urban settings are also seeking out traditional ceremonies and want to adhere to traditional Indian values. Unfortunately, many are confused as to what traditional Indian values truly are (for example, we see this in the commercialism in the modern-day powwow that Beaver decries). As Thornton points out, "Many present-day Indians would have trouble recognizing, let alone identifying with, the cultures of their ancestors (sic)."[11] Beaver encouraged us to learn from respected elders how to participate in our ceremonies properly. He was a great believer in time-honored procedures, and he believed that invocations in ceremonies should be guided by inspirations from the Creator, not our egos.

Many Indians suffer the effects of "Intergenerational Post Traumatic Stress" that has reduced the quality of life in many Indian communities. This Intergenerational P.T.S.D. is the result of the combined traumas of war, disease, enslavement, removal of Indian tribes from ancestral homelands, banning of Indian spiritual practices, the boarding school experience that broke up families and attempted to brain wash several generations, and the urban relocation programs of the mid-20th twentieth century, which lured reservation Indians to cities with false promises of good-paying jobs and adequate housing.

There are still high rates of alcoholism, impulsive acting out, and depression in some areas.[12] Indian psychologists argue that some emotionally troubled Indians suffer as a result of a lack of a positive Indian identity. It is argued that while they do not wish to be White, they see only suffering in being Indian. They identify with "Indian pain." It has been found that individuals who seek to develop a positive Indian identity by becoming actively involved in traditional ceremonies, such as the sweat lodge, show great improvement in the quality of their lives.[13] This clearly is what Beaver advocated.

Beaver lived up to the charge placed on him when he accepted his medicine pipe. He used it to help others. He did this in sweat lodge ceremonies, vision quests, pipe ceremonies, and Gourd Clan Societies, but most importantly in being a positive role model. He lived up to the admonitions of the great Lakota holy man Fools Crow to those who would use the pipe for good: "Become a clean hollow bone for the higher powers [by removing inner negativity]. ... Love everyone, put others first, be moral, keep your life in order. ... Have a clear self-image. ... Maintain a good sense of humor; it helps smooth the way in difficult times. ... As long as a holy person has the strength to do Wakan Tanka's will, we work at our job constantly. ... The greatest miracle is not something incredible, it is thousands of changed lives."[14] I particularly like the Lakota word for the Creator, "Wakan Tanka," which can be translated as "The Great Mystery." The spiritual road that Fools Crow, Beaver, and other American Indian holy persons walk is indeed strange and mysterious.

Beaver encouraged us to have faith in the Creator and in His ability to protect and heal us. He held that the Creator is not a respecter of individuals and that what He has done for Beaver, He will do for anyone who is willing to turn his or her life and will over to Him. Beaver wants us to know that God still creates miracles and will help us as long as we do the right thing for the right reason. He opens unseen pathways to success for those with faith. Beaver tells us that the traditional Indian way is not the only way but is the best way for the health and well-being of Indian people.

These are the teachings of a wise and loving heart.

Notes

1   Hightower, E. (1994). Influences of character-based coping style in psychological health. *Journal of Adult Development, 1*, 249–260.
2   Kobasa, S., Maddi, S., & Kahn, S. (1982). Hardiness and health: A prospective study. *Journal of Personality and Social Psychology, 42*, 168–177.

3 Lieberman, M., & Peskin, H. (1992). Adult life crises, in J. E. Birren, R. B. Sloane, and G. D. Cohen (Eds.), *Handbook of mental health and aging* (pp. 120–146). New York, NY: Academic Press.

Vaillant, G. (1977). *Adaptation to life: How the best and brightest come of age.* Boston, MA: Little Brown.

4 Haan, N., Millsap, R., & Hartka. (1986). As time goes by: Change and stability in personality over fifty years. *Psychology and Aging, 1,* 222–232.

Jahoda, M. (1958). *Concepts of positive mental health.* New York, NY: Basic Books.

5 Utter, J. (2001). *American Indians.* Norman, OK: University of Oklahoma Press.

6 Menchaca, M. (2001). *Recovering history, constructing race.* Austin, TX: University of Texas Press.

7 Brooks, J. (2002). *Confounding the color line.* Lincoln, NE: University of Nebraska Press.

8 Nagel, S. (December, 1995). American ethnic renewal. *American Sociological Review.*

9 Wilson, T. (1992). Blood quantum: Native American mixed bloods. In M. Root (Ed.), *Racially mixed people in America.* Newbury Park, CA: Sage.

10 Mause, M. *The present is past.* New York, NY: University Press.

11 Thornton, op cit.

12 Duran, E., & Duran, B. (1995). *Native American post-colonial psychology.* Albany, NY: SUNY Press.

13 Boone, J., & Blacklund, M. (1991). *A gathering of wisdoms: Tribal mental health.* La Conner, WA: Swinomish Tribal Council.

14 Mails, T. (1989). *Fools Crow: Wisdom and power.* Tulsa, OK: Council Oaks Books.

Afterword

I completed the first draft of this manuscript in July 2003. Beaver and I read it through together, and I asked him to clarify some of the comments that he had made in our interview. I made some revisions, and he approved the final draft of his statements presented here. There was more social science literature added to the book after Beaver's death.

This project began after Beaver requested that I help him put in print his beliefs about the proper way to approach Indian spirituality. I do not know why Beaver picked me to undertake this project. I can only say that we were very close, and I was happy to do this for him. I also felt he was a wise person and chronicling his views would be helpful to future generations. Beaver frequently said, "I am teaching you what my grandfathers taught me." I have tried throughout to be faithful to Beaver's actual statements.

I realize, looking back, that Beaver was giving me a final testimony of his life and teachings. I truly did not see this initially. It would have been too painful to contemplate his impending death. Beaver had stated to me on several occasions in the last 2 years of his life that he was "living on borrowed time." When Beaver moved back to Oklahoma in the summer of 2002, another Indian elder stated to me that

FIGURE A.1   **Beaver.**

Beaver was doing this because he wanted to die in his ancestral home. I dismissed this comment as overly sentimental. Beaver was a vigorous, active man, although he was 80. I thought that Beaver had many good years left to live.

Beaver came back to visit the Bay Area in November 2002. He had come out, in part, to speak in a class I was teaching on Native American Spirituality at UC Berkeley. While here, he also gourd danced and led prayer ceremonies. We went for a walk after sharing Thanksgiving dinner. Out of the blue, Beaver said to me that spirits had come to him and told him that he would soon be taken to the other side. I dismissed his comments as fanciful and assured him that he would live for many more years to come. Beaver smiled with that twinkle he frequently had in his eyes. He did not bother to debate or explain what he had said.

Beaver came out to visit California for the final time in June 2003, and he stayed at my home for much of that visit. He had come to give a public presentation at the Jung Institute of San Francisco on Indian spirituality. Beaver was in rare form and really wowed the audience that day. This trip was particularly inspiring to me, as only a couple of months before this talk, while clearing brush on the side of a hill at his sister's home in Oklahoma, Beaver lost his balance and tumbled down a hillside, fracturing his hip. He told me that the doctor who had treated him said he would be in a wheelchair for 6 months to a year. He told the doctor that the Creator would heal him a lot faster than that! I had encouraged Beaver to cancel his presentation, but, to my astonishment, he was walking normally by the time he arrived here. The doctor had reportedly told Beaver that the speed of this recovery was unprecedented, especially for a man of his age. He asked Beaver how this happened. Beaver said, "You're the doctor. You tell me." Beaver was comfortable and in good spirits during this final trip. While in the Bay Area, he led a prayer ceremony for a homeless Indian man who had been murdered by a White stranger—a hate crime.

Beaver and I spoke by phone weekly after his return to Oklahoma. The last time we spoke, we had an unusually long conversation: almost 3 hours. Looking back, it was as if he was clarifying several topics for me for a final time. I recall him saying it was important to trust God, even if it was His will to call you home. He said we should always have faith that God has good intentions for us.

The next day, I received a call from Beaver's son, Art, stating that Beaver had been seriously injured as a passenger in a car accident and had been airlifted to a trauma center in Tulsa. Like so many others, I prayed and fasted for Beaver's recovery. Unfortunately, he slipped away from us 3 days later on August 1, 2003. The night before he died, I was awakened by the plaintive sound of a wolf howling. I knew this was a sign to me that Beaver had made his transition; one of his closest spirit helpers was the Wolf.

I was very angry with God for a few days. I could not understand how he could let such a good man die in such a fashion. A gifted medicine person consoled me. He said that what Beaver had been telling me was literally true. He *had* been living on borrowed time. He said that the only reason Beaver had lived so long was that the Creator had indulged his desire to see some projects to completion. Now the Creator wanted him to go on to other, better things awaiting him. Hearing this helped me get over my anger and pick up my pipe for prayer again.

I prayed for Beaver to have a good transition to the other side. After I had performed the prayer ceremony, I saw Beaver in front of me for a second. He said, smiling, "I am all right, Gene." Several other people who were close to Beaver reported similar sightings.

After his death, Beaver's daughter-in-law, Rita, told me that Beaver had told her in the weeks before his death that the spirits had been coming to him more frequently to prepare him for his coming death. She said Beaver knew that his time on earth was coming to an end and was attempting to put things in order before his death.

I realize that many people, especially those who do not believe in Indian spiritual ways, will find what I have written above hard to accept. Beaver told me several times not to bother to explain these things to nonbelievers, as they cannot accept that these kinds of things happen. To these individuals, I would say believe at least this much: Beaver was a good and kind man who touched the lives of many. Most who met him felt they were better people for having known him.

Appendix

Questions for Classroom Discussion
and Reflection Papers

Chapter 1

1. What is historical trauma? How does a history of war, loss of tribal lands, decimation of Indian communities due to lack of immunity to European disease, poverty, children being taken from their families and placed in boarding schools far from home, and outlawing speaking Indian languages impact the morale and well-being of Indian people?

2. How do strongly held Indian cultural values—such as humility, cooperation, sharing, listening carefully to others, respecting the wisdom of elders, and caring for the natural environment—differ from the core values of mainstream American culture?

3. How do modern-day Indians vary on characteristics such as racial mixture, living on reservations or cities, being part of a federally recognized tribe, and identifying with tribal cultural values? What does it mean to have a traditional, bicultural, marginal, or assimilated American Indian identity? What is retraditionalization?

4. Why do you think a non-Indian visiting a traditional Indian community might face impersonal resentment or suspicion? How might practicing Indian etiquette—such as not interrupting others when they are speaking, asking permission before taking actions, or indicating a willingness to be teased and laugh with others—ease tensions?

5. The concept of the "empty center" suggests that counselors assessing the cultural identity of an Indian client must proceed with

some caution. Insecurities may be stirred up in such a discussion. How should the sensitive counselor proceed?

6. What is your ethnic background? Who gave you a sense of belonging to an ethnic group? Mention one comfort food or fun activity you associate with your family's ethnic heritage.

Chapter 2

1. What are the Choctaw words for God described in this chapter? How is "the path of the sun" described? What do all these various terms suggest to you about traditional Choctaw conceptions of the Divine?

2. Choctaw religious practices were shamanic in that priests and medicine men called upon spirit powers (such as the kwanokasha) for assistance and guidance. How might this approach have differed from the religious practices of Christian settlers in colonial America?

3. Did you know before reading this chapter that American Indians had to defend themselves from slave catchers in colonial America? Did you know that Indian and African slaves intermarried on Southern plantations? What do you think of this seldom discussed aspect of American history?

4. The early American government forced many Southern tribes to give up their prosperous homes and lands without compensation under the Indian Removal Act. Tribes such as the Choctaw were forced to walk from the Southeastern United States to the newly created Indian territory of Oklahoma in the Midwest. Many died on this "Trail of Tears." Was this fair? Do you feel the government of the United States owes the Choctaw (and other tribes forced to leave) an apology?

5. Did you know that in the early days of the American colonies, Indian nations were seen as separate governments that had as much standing with European powers as American settlers did? Do you think the power of American Indians diminished after the American Revolution and the creation of the United States?

Chapter 3

1. What did you learn about historical Choctaw communal social values, such as sharing, in this chapter?
2. Beaver's medicine man uncle was a man of integrity and generosity. Why do you think Whites and progressive Choctaw saw him as a bad person?
3. Beaver argues that adhering to traditional Indian cultural values is better proof that a person is Indian than the amount of Indian ancestry a person has. He argues that it does not matter if a person claiming Indian ancestry also has European, Asian, or African ancestry. Do you agree?
4. What is the difference between a "progressive" and a "traditional" Indian? How does the chapter indicate that the issue of adopting Euro American ways sometimes divides Indian communities?
5. Do you believe that a person living in the United States who claims he/she is Indian based on Indian ancestry from Mexican or Canadian tribes has a right to do so and be acknowledged as Indian?

Chapter 4

1. Do you feel the government was trying to help Indian children by sending them to boarding school or just trying to take over Indian communities through brainwashing?
2. How would you think the boarding school experience felt for Indian children and their families?
3. Do you believe that traumatic experiences such as child abuse can lead to alcoholism and drug addiction for some people?
4. Although he received a medal, Beaver indicates that being a combat veteran lead to a worsening of his substance abuse problem and emotional stability. Why do you think this occurred? How do combat veterans cope with Post Traumatic Stress Disorder?
5. Do you think Beaver's mental health was further damaged by his wife abandoning him after the war? You may recall that his mother died when he was a child. He also lost much family contact as a teen after he went to boarding school. In short, how did multiple losses impact Beaver's emotional state?

Chapter 5

1. Many question why the federal government took away the tribal recognition of several Indian nations in the 1950s under the Termination Act. Some suggest that many Whites had thought American Indian tribes would have ceased to exist by the 1900's and now wanted the government to get out of treaty agreements that had no end in sight. Some treaties promised money and retention of tribal lands "for as long as the grass will grow." They argued that these treaties were originally created to settle Indian wars that were unlikely in the 20th century, therefore, breaking these agreements was acceptable. However, the proponents of Termination Program argued that its purpose was only to encourage prosperity for Indians by forcing them to adapt to mainstream American life. What do you think?

2. Why do you think laws were passed forbidding Indians to practice their traditional religions? They could be arrested and punished. Should we have needed passage of the American Indian Religious Freedom Act in order for Indians to again be able practice their traditional religious ways? Religious freedom is protected in the U.S. Constitution.

3. Prior to contact with Christian missionaries, most American Indian tribes were accepting of people who chose to live as other than their biological gender. They also were accepting of homosexual activity in some form. Do you think the American Indian Two Spirit movement seen in cities is a reflection of the modern Gay liberation movement, a return to traditional ways, or both?

4. Many Indians moved to cities under the Urban Relocation Act. What are some things Indians did in urban areas such as San Francisco to adjust to city life?

5. How do you think the Urban Indian community might differ from tribal reservations? Is the Urban Indian a new kind of intertribal American Indian?

Chapter 6

1. We have discussed the fact that American Indian cultural values are much more collective and communal than Euro American individualistic values. This can be seen in the way Beaver helped others. Please

discuss Beaver's taking in a homeless child at the beginning of this chapter and the narrative in which a pregnant young woman with two children in tow comes to Beaver's treatment program for help. What are the clinical advantages and risks to his approach?

2. Beaver discusses substance abuse treatment in terms of both abstinence (not using alcohol and drugs) and sobriety (resolving personal conflicts to the point of no longer wanting to abuse alcohol or drugs). Do you think one approach is better than the other? Or should they be combined in some way?

3. In American Indian communities, there is often a prohibition against using drugs and alcohol at public social events. Based on the reading in this chapter, why is this the case?

4. Alcoholics Anonymous Announcement encourages people in recovery to seek a "Higher Power" to help them stay sober. Beaver actively tried to help Indian clients to find this Higher Power in American Indian ceremonial practices. He was open to non-Indians participating if they were open to Indian ways. The federal government eventually refused to pay for treatment of non-Indians at his program. Do you feel the government was justified in doing this?

5. What does Beaver say helped him become free of addiction to drugs and alcohol?

Chapter 7

1. What is the true role of the warrior, as described by Beaver? Is it like the Indian warrior portrayed in Hollywood films?

2. American Indians place a high value on Nature and God as revealed through plants, animals, stones, etc. Beaver said, "Nature is my church." What do you think he meant by this?

3. Beaver indicates that many non-Indians would have trouble participating in Indian ceremonies such as the sweat lodge due to differences in how Indians see time (e.g., questions like "When will we start and end the ceremony?"). How different is this attitude from the way most therapists conduct therapy? Indians do not place a high value on timeliness. Things start when all are ready. How do you think about time and schedules? Can a non-Indian successfully enter a sweat lodge, or any other Indian ceremony?

4. It has been said that "Euro Americans look for good ideas to run their lives by, while Indians seek visions." After reading this chapter on prayer, meditation, sweat lodges, pipe ceremonies, and visions quests, how would you interpret this saying?

5. Indians believe in the power of prayer to heal others. They believe God and His helpers can do many helpful things. Do you believe in the world of spiritual assistance, as described in this chapter? If not, how would you communicate with an Indian who does believe in such things in a respectful manner?

Chapter 8

1. Do you believe a person can overcome a difficult childhood? What evidence is presented for this from research on positive mental health?

2. What experiences in his life may have caused Beaver to stress the importance of Indians remaining proud of their culture?

3. Why did Beaver stress the importance of the Indian people working together, whatever their tribal and racial mixtures, in urban settings?

4. After reading this book, what do you see as the role of medicine people and spiritual elders in helping the Indian community overcome historical trauma and PTSD?

5. Are you willing to accept and express yourself? Do you judge others by who they are, not what they are? Do you believe we are all meant to help each other find joy, as Beaver stated?